THE DELICIOUS

CHAR GRILLER

GRILL & SMOKER COOKBOOK

1000-DAY DELICIOUS BBQ RECIPES FOR BEGINNERS AND ADVANCED MASTERS

AUDREY GARCIA

CONTENTS

INTRODUCTION

What Exactly Are Wood Pellets?

Wood pellets are made from a combination of hardwood shavings and sawdust. This is pressurized, compressed down, and held together through the use of the wood's lignin, an all-natural binding agent. It's made into long, pencil-thick rods that are broken into smaller pieces. Most wood pellet pieces will be about a half-inch long.

During the compression of the wood shaving and sawdust mixture, most of the air and moisture is removed. Also, this mixture means you won't be burning any bark, dirt, etc that you would find on raw wood logs. This results in an extremely efficient and clean-burning fuel source. Pellets used for smoking are also food-grade. Therefore, they do not contain any adhesives or chemicals. They also don't contain softwoods, like pine or spruce, that have a high amount of sap that can adversely affect the taste of your meat.

Most wood pellets are made up of mainly oak, a very stable burning wood. This is then blended with another hardwood or fruitwood to impart the flavor through the smoke.

The Operation Principle of Char Griller Wood Pellet Grill

Wood pellet grills use an auger that moves the hardwood pellets from the hopper to the fire pot underneath the grill. The higher the set temperature, the more pellets are dispensed into the auger. Once in the fire pot, a hot rod ignites the pellets creating a fire, then a fan stokes the fire creating convection heat to evenly cook your food in the grill. A drip tray sits over the fire pot, keeping the direct flames off your food while catching food drippings to help prevent flare-ups.

The Advantages of Your Char Griller Wood Pellet Grill

1. The Char Griller wood pellet grill makes barbecuing easy.

Plug it in, fill the hopper with BBQ pellets, turn it on, set the temperature, and let the grill do the rest. Pellet grills are designed to allow one to take a hands-off approach to cooking by letting a controller do the majority of the work.

You don't need to haul logs or arrange charcoal. You can put away the lighter fluid and flint. The Ignition sequence on a pellet grill starts with a single button press.

Once the ignition sequence is complete, the controller's capabilities determine to what extent it is able to control the cooking process. Pellet grill controllers have evolved over time from simple low, medium, & high setting devices to the advanced controllers found on high end pellet grills today.

The programs and algorithms that comprise its firmware were designed by us to ensure peak performance, consistency, and accuracy whether you're grilling steaks in the sub-zero Alaskan winter or smoking a brisket all day in the blistering deserts of Arizona.

This level of control also allows you to choose cook length, temperature, and when that temperature should change. You're in control and can fully customize the longest and most complicated of cooks to your exact specifications.

Add to this the convenience of technologies like Wi-Fi and BlueTooth and it's easy to see the appeal of the work smarter, not harder approach to smoking and grilling meat.

2. The Char Griller wood pellet grill is safe.

Gas can explode. Charcoal and wood logs are messy and can smolder for days after use. Direct cooking over fire increases the likelihood of flare ups and grease fires.

Pellet grills cook indirectly, meaning no open flame, flying sparks, or direct contact between fat drippings and fire. MAK Pellet grills create small, precisely controlled fires in a stainless-steel firepot. This firepot is surrounded by a stainless-steel body and covered by a stainless-steel diffuser, and drip pan at a minimum.

Pellets are released in small quantities and consumed completely. As long as you maintain relatively minimal cleaning routines, which we make as easy as possible by using a removable firepot, the chances of anything out of the ordinary happening are extremely low.

The pellet grill is the safest outdoor cooking device ever invented.

3.Pellet grilling is better for your health and the environment. No added oils or fats are needed to achieve the tremendous flavor that cooking on a pellet grill imparts. You're cooking with real wood, which means you're using a fuel that has been used since the dawn of time. Because you are cooking indirectly, excess animal fat drippings are not burned up and made carcinogenic by open flame. Instead, they hit a grease pan and convert to gases which help flavor your food. Hardwood BBQ pellets burn with a more than 98% efficiency. This reduces the exposure of carcinogenic substances and HCA's to you and the environment. Avoiding the creation of carcinogenic smoke is not only good for your health. Extremely low particulate matter means fresher, safer air to breathe. Barbecue pellets reduce landfill disposal of sawdust by millions of tons per year. Barbecue pellets are not only a sustainable biofuel, they are also the ultimate example of re-purposing.

Tips for Using Your Char Griller Wood Pellet Grill

1. Season your new pellet grill.

Season your new pellet grill according to the manufacturer's directions (a process that usually takes 45 minutes to one hour). This burns off any residual oils from the manufacturing process.

2. Allow yourself some time to get acquainted with your new grill/smoker.

Allow yourself some time to get acquainted with your new grill/smoker. We know you'll be anxious to try it out, but don't be overly ambitious. Instead of a whole brisket, which could take 15 hours or more, or a budget-busting prime rib roast, start with chicken (parts, such as breasts or wings, or a whole bird), pork loin tenderloin, or blade (shoulder) steaks, Cornish hens, salmon steaks or fillets, or other relatively inexpensive cuts that can be completed in 2 hours or less.

3. Identify any hot spots—most grills have them.

Identify any hot spots—most grills have them. Preheat your grill to medium-high as directed by the owner's manual, then lay slices of cheap white bread shoulder to shoulder across the grate. Watch carefully, then flip after a few minutes. Take a photo of the results. The darkest bread will indicate where the temperature might be hotter. (Print the photo out and add it to your owner's manual for reference.)

4. Don't let your meat come to room temperature before cooking.

Whatever meat you select, put it on the preheated grill/smoker straight from the refrigerator. Do not, as many recipes suggest, allow it to come to room temperature before cooking.

As Steven often notes, high-end steak houses do not leave their meats out at room temperature. (The danger area is 40 to 140 degrees.) The heat of the grill is sufficient to raise the internal temperature of the meat by those few degrees.

5. Invest in a good meat thermometer.

A laser-type thermometer such as this one will give you a more accurate temperature reading at grill level than a built-in dome thermometer. Determine the temperature range of your grill model from lowest to highest (180 degrees to 500+, for example).

Cleaning Your Char Griller Wood Pellet Grill

For spot-cleaning the outside of your grill, you can simply use a dry cloth to remove grease marks, dust and dirt quickly. To perform a deep clean, use a soft cloth with soap and water, stainless steel cleaner or a bbq degreaser. Follow these steps to clean the outside of your BBQ:

1. Make sure your grill is cold before spraying any cleaner on the outside of your grill.
2. Apply your cleaner using a soft cloth or spray bottle. If spraying cleaner onto your pellet grill, be very careful not to get any inside of your grill. Avoid spraying stainless steel cleaner onto plastic components as it can cause them to degrade more quickly.
3. Allow the cleaner to sit for at least 30 seconds to break down any dried grease or food residue.
4. Wipe the cleaner off with a clean cloth or paper towel. If cleaning a stainless steel BBQ, wipe in the same direction as the grain. If your smoker has a painted surface, wipe in circles.
5. Repeat this process as necessary until all of the dirt and grime is removed.
6. Using a wet cloth, wipe down the surface of the grill to remove all remaining cleaner or soap residue. Do not rinse your pellet grill with a hose or bucket as water can get into the grill or hopper and cause damage its electrical components or ruin the pellets.

Always unplug your pellet grill from its power source before cleaning it with water or liquid cleaner and allow it to dry for at least 24 hours before your next grilling session. Empty your wood pellets from the hopper before cleaning and check that there is no water or cleaner in the hopper before putting the pellets back in.

POULTRY

Fried Chicken And Corn

Cooking Time: 10 Min

Ingredients:

- 2 C. flour
- 2 oz. corn starch
- 2 oz. paprika
- 1 Tbsp. cinnamon
- Salt & pepper to taste
- 4 ears of corn
- 4 oz. melted unsalted butter
- 1 Tbsp. paprika

Directions:

1. Soak chicken up to 24 hours in buttermilk and hot sauce
2. In a bowl mix corn starch, salt & pepper, cinnamon, and paprika
3. Mix ingredients well
4. Add chicken to mixture and coat thoroughly
5. Once coated, let sit for 30 minutes
6. Heat grill to 375°F
7. In a hot cast iron skillet, add chicken and oil
8. Cook chicken 3-5 minutes per side
9. Soak corn in saltwater for up to 24 hours
10. Boil them in butter water for 10 minutes before adding to grill
11. On a plate, mix paprika, salt, pepper, and melted butter
12. Mix and roll corn and cover with mixture
13. Add to grill and cook for 3-5 minutes

2-burner Flat Iron Seasoned Chicken Breasts

Cooking Time: 20 Min

Ingredients:

- 4 Boneless Chicken Breasts
- 1/4 Cup of Extra Virgin Olive Oil
- 1 Lemon
- 1 Tbsp of Garlic Powder
- 1 Tbsp of Onion Powder
- 1 Tbsp of Italian Seasoning or choice of herbs
- 1 Tbsp of Char-Griller Lemon Pepper Rub
- 1 Tsp of Cayenne Pepper

Directions:

1. If you prefer to rinse your chicken breasts, do so in cold water. Pat completely dry with paper towels. In a resealable bag add olive oil, and all herbs and seasonings. Add chicken and seal the bag before mixing until all pieces are thoroughly coated. Place the bag(s) in the refrigerator for 1 hour-overnight. With Flat Iron preheated to medium heat, add chicken breast and generous squirt of water to the cooktop before covering with the Char-Griller Basting Dome. Keeping covered, allow it to cook for 9-10 minutes. Remove Basting Dome and generously squeeze juice from lemon over each chicken breast. Allow chicken to cook uncovered for 5-6 more minutes, letting water to evaporate and slight crusting to form on bottom before flipping once more. Cook chicken until the internal temperature reaches 165°F. Serve immediately. Enjoy!

Turkey Tips

Cooking Time: 3½ Hrs

Ingredients:

- 7-8 lb. turkey breast, cubed
- 1 medium onion, thinly sliced
- Chicken BBQ rub
- BBQ sauce
- 1-2 Tbsp. butter
- Salt and pepper, to taste

Directions:

1. Place turkey in a large roasting pan in an even layer, add BBQ sauce and turn to evenly coat. Allow to marinate for an hour.
2. Pre-heat grill to 230°F. Place pan with turkey on the grill and smoke for 30 minutes per pound or until internal temperature reaches 165°F.
3. While turkey is smoking, place a cast iron skillet on the grill and heat until very hot.
4. Remove turkey from roasting pan and add to skillet with onions, butter and more BBQ sauce. Allow to smoke for an additional 25 minutes, stirring occasionally.

Smoked Chicken Thighs

Cooking Time: 1 Hrs

Ingredients:

- 7 lbs bone in, skin on chicken quarters
- 1 C. apple cider vinegar
- 1/2 C. extra virgin olive oil
- 1/2 C. extra virgin olive oil
- 1/2 C. minced onion
- 1 1/2 Tsp. kosher salt
- 4 minced garlic cloves

Directions:

1. Mix apple cider vinegar, extra virgin olive oil, minced onion, kosher salt, and garlic cloves in a bowl 2. Pour mixture over chicken.
2. Set in fridge for at least an hour
3. Heat grill to 250°F
4. Add Smokin' Stone 6. Place chicken on grill 7. To crisp up the skin, take temp up to 350°-400°F when chicken has internal temp of 140°F for about 15 minuets 8. Remove chicken when internal temp reaches 165°-185°F
5. Let cool for 10 minutes, then serve.

Smoked Turkey Breast

Ingredients:

- 1 Turkey Breast (Thawed)
- 10-12 Cups of cold water
- 1/2 Cup of Kosher Salt
- 1/4 Cup of Brown Sugar
- 1/4 Cup of Extra Virgin Olive Oil
- 1 Tbsp of Chili Powder
- 1 Tbsp of Paprika
- 1 Tbsp of Garlic Powder
- 1 Tbsp of Ground Black pepper
- 1/2 Tbsp of Seasoning Salt

Directions:

1. Mix all the brine ingredients (2-4) in a large container. Submerge the turkey breast and allow it to marinate for 8 hours up to overnight. Remove from the brine and pat dry with paper towels. You may refrigerate for an extra 2 hours to allow skin to completely dry. Preheat your smoker to 225°F. Coat the exterior of your turkey with the olive oil before massaging in the rest of the seasonings and spices ingredients (5-10). Add the turkey to the smoker, breast side up. Smoke until the internal temp reaches about 150°F. This should take about 2 hours. Increase the temperature to about 500-550°F for about 5 minutes to allow skin to crisp up until the internal temperature reaches 165°F. Allow the turkey to rest for 20-30 minutes before carving. Enjoy!

Pulled Chicken Crunch Wrap Style Burritos

Cooking Time: 10 Min

Ingredients:

- 1 Cup of Pulled Chicken Mixed with Taco Seasoning and Enchilada Sauce
- 2 Large Burrito Sized Tortillas
- 2 Corn Tostadas, Or Tortillas You Crisp In The Oven
- 2 Small flour tortilla
- 1 Cup Shredded Lettuce
- 1/2 Cup Pico De Gallo, Or Chopped Tomatoes
- 1/2 Cup Queso
- 1/2 Cup Shredded Cheese
- 1/2 Cup Sour Cream

Directions:

1. Place large tortilla on a flat surface, add half of the chicken mixture and half of the queso. Top with a tostada and half of the sour cream. Sprinkle on half the lettuce, pico, and shredded cheese, and top with the remaining small tortilla. Fold inward over the small tortilla to close and repeat the same process to finish the second crunch wrap.
2. Preheat Char-Griller Flat Iron Griddle over medium heat. Drizzle with 1 tsp oil, and spread evenly. Place Crunch Wraps seam side down on the griddle and cook for about 5 minutes until golden brown. Flip, and cook for another 5 minutes until the other side is golden brown. Serve while hot and enjoy!

Chicken Cordon Bleu

Cooking Time: 20 Min

Ingredients:

- 2-3 Chicken breasts
- 6 strips of bacon
- 2 slices deli ham
- 4 slices of cheese
- Jalapeños, seeded and sliced, optional
- Garlic powder
- Salt and pepper, to taste

Directions:

1. Rinse chicken breasts and pat dry with paper towel. Place inside a resealable plastic bag and flatten using a mallet, until about a ½" thick. 2. Remove chicken from bag and layer a slice of ham and 2 slices of cheese on each. Place jalapeño slices on each, if desired. 3. Tightly roll chicken breast, keeping ham and cheese inside. Wrap each breast with 3 slices of bacon and lightly season with garlic powder, salt and pepper on both sides, to taste. Refrigerate for 10-20 minutes. 4. Pre-heat grill to 400°F and place chicken directly on grates, for about 20 minutes, flipping halfway through for good sear marks. Chicken is done when internal temperature reaches 165°F.
2. Slice, serve and enjoy!

Grilled Nachos

Cooking Time: 25-30 Min

Ingredients:

- 3 boneless skinless chicken breasts
- 6 mini sweet peppers
- 1 bag of tortilla chips
- 1 8oz. bag of shredded fiesta cheese
- 1 jar of your favorite salsa
- Original All-Purpose BBQ rub, or your favorite rub

Directions:

1. Heat grill to 325°F.
2. While grill is heating, rub the chicken breasts liberally with your favorite rub or use Original All-Purpose BBQ rub, to taste.
3. Place chicken breasts on the grill and cook for 6 minutes per side until internal temperature reaches 165°F, flipping halfway through for good sear marks.
4. Remove chicken and chop into chunks. Chop up sweet peppers.
5. In a grill safe pan, layer chips, chicken, peppers and cheese for three layers.
6. Place pan on the grill and grill for 12-15 minutes.
7. Once cheese is melted, remove from the grill and top with your favorite salsa.
8. Enjoy!

Grilled Chicken And Broccoli Stir-fry

Cooking Time: 10 Min

Ingredients:

- 1 lb. chicken breast
- 8 oz. bottle Italian dressing
- 1 Tbsp. extra-virgin olive oil
- 1 head broccoli, stemmed and cut into florets
- ½ red pepper, sliced
- ½ green pepper, sliced
- ½ yellow pepper, sliced
- ½ red onion, sliced
- 1 Tbsp. dried basil
- 1 Tbsp. dried oregano
- 1 Tbsp. garlic powder
- Olive oil, for brushing
- Salt and pepper, to taste

Directions:

1. Rinse chicken and pat dry with paper towel. Pour Italian dressing into a large resealable plastic bag, add chicken and gently shake to evenly coat. Marinate for 2–3 hours in the refrigerator, or best overnight.
2. Rinse produce and pat dry with paper towel. Pre-heat grill to 400°F and brush a grill wok with olive oil.
3. Remove chicken from marinade, cut into 1" thick strips and place in grill wok. Discard dressing.
4. Sear the chicken strips evenly on all sides, until golden brown, for about 3 minutes.
5. Add the broccoli, red pepper, green pepper, yellow pepper, and red onion to the wok and cook for about 5 minutes, stirring occasionally.
6. Mix together basil, oregano and garlic powder in a small bowl to make seasoning and add salt and pepper, to taste. Sprinkle over chicken and vegetables and stir to combine.
7. Serve over cooked rice and garnish with fresh basil and chopped cashews or peanuts, if desired.

Asian Chicken Salad

Cooking Time: 25 Min

Ingredients:

- 4 Cups Mixed Greens
- 2-3 Chicken Breasts
- 1/2 Cup Chopped Carrots
- 1/2 Cup Chopped Cucumber
- 1/2 Cup Chopped Radish
- 1/2 Cup Chopped Cilantro
- 1 Cup Cooked Quinoa
- 1/2 Cup Crispy Wonton Strips
- 1/2 Cup Soy Sauce (Marinade)
- 1/2 Cup Rice Wine Vinegar (Marinade)
- 1/4 Cup Sesame Oil
- 2 Tbsp Chili Garlic Paste or Sriracha
- 2 Tbsp Honey

Directions:

1. Whisk ingredients for marinade and reserve half.
2. Add 2-3 chicken breasts to the remaining marinade and let it sit for at least 30 mins.
3. While your chicken is marinating, preheat your Char-Griller to high heat, scraping your grates to keep your chicken from sticking! Grill chicken for 10-12 mins per side, until inside temp reaches 165. Let rest 10 mins before slicing.
4. Add chicken to a bed of mixed greens with an assortment of veggies the remaining veggies, and pro-tip: I always have a bag of crispy wonton strips in the pantry, so add those for a delicious crunch! Divide the dressing in half and store with the salad for a quick & easy week day lunch!"

Easy Chicken And Cheese Quesadillas

Cooking Time: 10 Min

Ingredients:

- Pack Of Soft Tortillas
- 2 Lbs Chicken Tenderloin
- Your Choice of Cheese
- Your Choice Of Other Toppings

Directions:

1. Bring your griddle to high / medium-high heat, throw down some oil and cook up your chicken. Once they are cooked and chopped up, move them off to the side.
2. Throw down a little more oil because the griddle may be pretty dry by now, then a couple of tortillas to brown and soften up.
3. After flipping the tortillas once, add your toppings. Start with cheese all over the tortillas, then add your other toppings only on one half of the tortilla.
4. Fold the tortilla in half to create your quesadilla. Press firmly to activate the 'cheese glue'.
5. Flip once more to ensure everything is melty goodness inside.
6. Cut with a pizza cutter and serve with your choice of dips!

Smoked Carolina Turkey

Ingredients:

- 10-12 lb. turkey
- 3 Tbsp. red pepper flakes
- ¼ C. paprika
- ¼ C. ground mustard
- ½ C. brown sugar
- 2 Tbsp. coarse black pepper
- 2 Tbsp. Kosher salt
- 2 Tbsp. melted butter

Directions:

1. Pour melted butter over turkey, or use marinade injector to inject butter into turkey
2. Mix red pepper flakes, paprika, ground mustard, brown sugar, black pepper and salt in small bowl to create seasoning mix
3. Rub turkey all over with seasoning mix
4. Place turkey on grill over indirect heat at 250°F or use Smokin' Stone
5. Inject turkey with its own juices every other hour
6. Cook time is 1 hour per pound or until turkey reaches internal temp of 165°F

Chicken Lollipops By Jeremy Souza

Ingredients:

- Chicken Drumsticks
- Favorite Seasoning
- Favorite Sauce or Glaze
- Charcoal
- Smoking Wood Chunks

Directions:

1. Transform the drumsticks into lollipops Using a sharp knife and kitchen shears cut around the chicken ankle to create the handle Remove the skin, meat, tendons, and cartilage to expose the bone. This will be your "lollipop stick" Remove any loose tendons with the kitchen shears To ensure that the chicken legs will stand up straight, flatten the bottoms with a sharp cleaver Cover the chicken leg handles with foil to protect from burning and discoloration Season the chicken liberally with your favorite seasoning. We decided to go with a habanero seasoning to pair with a sweet apricot glaze to come later Preheat your grill or smoker and set it up for 2 Zone Cooking (Direct and Add any smoking chunks or chips at this point if you wish Place the chicken on your grill away from the direct heat and allow to cook and smoke until an internal temperature of 165*F is reached At this point it's time to sauce! Use your favorite sauce and coat each drumstick Return to the smoker and cook for an additional 10 minutes Remove from the smoker and glaze one last time until they're nice and saucy Remove the foil, plate them nicely on a platter and enjoy. These are sure to impress!

Creole Latin Spatchcock Turkey

Cooking Time: 1-2 Hrs

Ingredients:

- Whole turkey
- Kitchen Scissors & Pairing Knife
- Char-Griller Marinade Injector
- Creole Seasoning: Generous Coating
- Sazón Seasoning: Generous Coating
- Adobo Seasoning
- Garlic Powder
- Onion Powder
- Creole Butter Injectable Marinade (17 Oz)
- Fresh or Dry Cilantro
- Olive Oil
- Turkey Oven Bags
- Bucket Or Cooler
- Char-Griller Grill

Directions:

1. Chop up fresh cilantro and set aside.

2. Remove turkey from bag & remove everything inside the cavity area along with the plastic tie holding the legs. 3.Using kitchen scissors & pairing knife remove the backbone to Spatchcock the turkey. Also trim and remove any access fat & skin.

3. Flip Turkey breast side up & push down on the breast using both hands to help flatten the turkey.

4. Inject turkey with Creole Butter. Use any extra Creole & rub on breast under skin.

5. Generously add olive to the both sides of the turkey.Tip: continue to trim access fat & skin as you go along.

6. Generously season the turkey with Adobo, Sazón, Creole, onion powder & garlic powder. Then sprinkle cilantro 8. Place turkey in turkey/oven bag & place in bucket or cooler. Place in refrigerator & allow the turkey to rest for 12-24 hours. Cooking Directions 1. Remove turkey from bucket/cooler & allow to rest at room temperature for 1-2 hours. 2. Preheat your Char-griller Smoker to 240°. 3. Place turkey in smoker and smoke until the turkey reaches 165° internal temperature. Product tip: use the Char-griller remote thermometer or folding prob thermometer. 4. Check on turkey about every hour & baste turkey with butter & spritz with apple juice. Tip: rotate turkey in different directions to allow even cooking. 5. After turkey reaches 165° internal temperature allow the turkey to rest for a minimum of 25 minutes. Sprinkle additional cilantro. 7. Slice, serve & enjoy.

Curried Chicken Skewers

Cooking Time: 10-12 Min

Ingredients:

- 3-4 lb. chicken tenders
- 2 Tbsp. vegetable oil
- 2 Tbsp. yellow mustard
- 2 Tbsp. honey
- 2 Tbsp. curry powder
- 1 Tsp. salt
- ½ Tsp. garlic powder
- ½ Tsp. pepper
- ½ Tsp. allspice

Directions:

1. Soak the bamboo skewers in water for 15 minutes, so they don't burn on the grill.
2. While skewers are soaking, rinse the chicken tenders and pat dry with paper towel.
3. Combine oil, mustard, honey, curry powder, garlic powder, allspice, salt and pepper in a medium bowl to make curry seasoning and mix well. Add chicken, turning to coat evenly and skewer.
4. Place skewered chicken tenders on the grill at 375°F for 10 minutes, until internal temperature reaches 165°F.

Beer Soda Can Chicken

Cooking Time: 1.5 Hrs

Ingredients:

- Olive Oil
- Chicken BBQ rub
- Favorite beer/soda

Directions:

1. 4.5 lb whole chicken
2. Cover chicken in olive oil
3. Season the whole chicken on both sides with Chicken BBQ rub, or your favorite poultry rub
4. Open your favorite beer/soda can
5. Place inside the beer can chicken rack
6. Place chicken over the can on the rack
7. Pre-heat grill to 350°F
8. Add Smokin' Stone
9. Place drip pan on Smokin' Stone and add more beer/soda and lemons
10. Cook for about an hour and a half 11. Remove when internal temp reaches 165°F

PIZZA

Flat-iron Pizza Quesadillas

Cooking Time: 10 Min

Ingredients:

- 8 Flour Tortillas
- 1 Pack Of Pepperoni And Or Salami
- 2 Cups Of Mozzarella Cheese
- 4 Tbsp Of Butter Or Margarine
- 2 Cups Of Spaghetti Sauce
- 4 Tbsp Of Dried Basil And Or Oregano

Directions:

1. Heat Flat Iron to medium heat. Add butter to flat top and spread across allowing it to melt. Once heated, place 4 tortillas flat on top. Immediately layer cheese, oregano/basil, meat and more cheese on the tortilla. Top with another tortilla. (Optionally, you can make each tortilla its own mini-quesadilla by only layering meat and cheese on one half then folding it in half.) Allow the cheese to fully melt on the inside before using a spatula to flip each over, adding more butter to the flat top, if necessary. Once cheese is melted and tortillas are browned and crisped to your liking, remove from Flat Iron. Serve each quesadilla with spaghetti sauce for dipping. Enjoy!

Gravity 980 Grilled Pizza

Cooking Time: 12 Min

Ingredients:

- 1 Lb. Fresh Pizza Dough
- 1/4 Cup of Extra Virgin Olive Oil
- All Purpose White Flour
- 1 Cup of Fresh Mozzarella Cheese
- Optional Toppings: Pepperoni, Vegetables, Sausage, Bacon, etc.

Directions:

1. Remove the fire shutter from your Gravity 980, load and light the hopper, then preheat to 500-600°F. Add flour to your counter or cutting board before prepping your dough into the desired pizza shape. Add pizza sauce, olive oil and cheese then add your pizza to the pizza stone. Add any toppings that must be cooked then add to the grill. Cook the pizza for 8-12 minutes or until desired brownness. Add any remaining fresh toppings and serve immediately. Enjoy!

Meat Lovers Pizza

Cooking Time: 9 To 12 Min

Ingredients:

- Pre-made Pizza Dough
- Pizza Sauce
- Garlic Powder - 2 tsp
- Shredded Mozzarella - 1 to 1.5 Cups
- 8 to 10 Slices of Pepperoni
- 1-2 Slices of Ham - Chopped
- 1/2 Cup Spicy Sausage - Browned
- 1/2 Cup Ground Beef - Browned
- Parmesan Cheese - Grated
- 1/2 Cup Arugula
- Olive Oil - 1 Tbs
- Salt and Pepper to Taste

Directions:

1. This Meat Lover's pizza packs on the flavor with ham, spicy sausage, ground beef, pepperoni, and two types of cheese. The optional arugula can take it over the top with its peppery bite. Cook this hot and fast on the AKORN for restaurant quality crust.
2. Allow pizza dough to come up to room temperature (about 8 hours). Tip: Place Pizza Dough in a large plastic bag that seals for the best results.
3. Brown ground beef and spicy sausage. Set aside.
4. Preheat AKORN to 500-600 degrees Fahrenheit. Insert Smokin' Stone. Place Pizza Stone on grates to heat.
5. Shape dough into pizza on a cutting board covered in semolina.
6. Add desired amount of pizza sauce and garlic powder.
7. Add ground beef and sausage to pizza. Add pepperoni and ham. Add mozzarella cheese.
8. Add parmesan cheese to taste.
9. Place pizza on pizza stone. Close lid and cook for 9 minutes or until crust is crisp and cheese melted.
10. Remove from pizza stone and allow to rest for 5 minutes.
11. Toss arugula with olive oil, salt and pepper.
12. Top pizza with arugula if desired.

Grilled Caprese Pizza

Cooking Time: 6 To 8 Min

Ingredients:

- 1 Ball of Pizza Dough, Rolled out Thinly
- 1/2 Cup Pesto
- 1 Small Ball Fresh Mozzarella, Torn to Shreds
- 1/2 Cup Cherry Tomatoes, Halved
- 4-5 Fresh Basil Leaves, Whole or Torn
- 1 Tbsp Fresh Parsley, Chopped
- 1 Tbsp Fresh Parmesan, Shredded or Grated
- 2 Tbsp Olive Oil
- Salt & Pepper to Taste

Directions:

1. Preheat Char-Griller to high heat. Scrape and oil your grates well so the dough does not stick.
2. Spread 1 T of oil to one side of the dough, and place oiled side down on heat first. Immediately turn burners to low and let dough cook for 2-3 minutes that side, until dough bubbles up.
3. Brush remaining oil on uncooked side, and then carefully use spatula to flip dough over. Turn heat off.
4. Spread the dough evenly with pesto, and scatter the torn mozzarella and halved tomatoes over the top. Close the lid, and allow residual heat from the grill to finish cooking the pizza for 5 minutes.
5. Remove pizza from heat and add fresh basil, parsley, and grated parmesan. Serve while warm. Enjoy!

Fire-grilled Pizza

Cooking Time: 10-15 Min

Ingredients:

- 3 C. bread flour
- 2 Tsp. salt
- 3 Tbsp. vegetable oil
- 1 Tsp. sugar
- 1 packet rapid-rising yeast
- 1 C. water
- Corn meal, for dusting
- Tomato sauce
- Garlic powder
- Cheese, if desired
- Toppings of choice

Directions:

1. In a stand mixer fitted with a dough hook, add water and yeast to the bowl and mix well. Then add sugar, salt and vegetable oil and mix.
2. Add bread flour, 1 C. at a time, and mix until a dough forms. Add water as needed to keep dough from sticking to the sides of the bowl. 3. Remove dough and knead for 1 minute by hand, forming it into a ball. Lightly spray a bowl with cooking spray, add dough ball and lightly spray the top. Cover with plastic wrap and allow dough to rise for 1 hour, until doubled in size.
3. Note: Dough is enough to make 2 medium pizzas. Cut dough in half, wrap unused portion and refrigerate or freeze for later use.
4. Pizza
5. Lightly flour counter. Stretch and work dough by hand, kneading until a 12" circle forms. Transfer dough to a wooden pizza peel lightly dusted with corn meal, to prevent sticking. 2. Pre-heat grill to 450°F. Sprinkle pizza dough with garlic powder. Spoon a layer of tomato sauce in the center and spread around to edges of dough. 3. Sprinkle a layer of cheese on top, if desired. Place other toppings on top of cheese layer. 4. Place pizza on pizza stone and allow pizza to cook for 10-15 minutes with lid closed. Rotate pizza after 5 minutes to ensure even cooking. Remove pizza from grill and allow to rest for 4-5 minutes. Slice and enjoy!

Breakfast Pizza

Cooking Time: 10 To 12 Min

Ingredients:

- Pre-made Pizza Dough
- Sun-dried Tomatoes - 1 Cup
- 1 Fresh Mozzarella Ball
- Deli Ham - 4 slices
- 1 Egg
- 1 (8 oz) Jar Tomato Sauce
- Baby Spinach - 2 Cups
- Dried Basil to Taste
- Salt and Pepper to Taste
- Semolina
- Garlic Powder to Taste

Directions:

1. Allow pre-made pizza dough to sit at room temperature covered with a clean dishcloth for at least 6 hours.
2. Preheat grill to medium high heat
3. Add pizza stone to grill and allow to preheat
4. Spread out pre-made pizza dough on a cutting board covered with semolina
5. Cut up ham and spinach.
6. Cut mozzarella into thin slices
7. Add tomato sauce to pizza. (As much as desired.)
8. Season with Garlic Salt and Basil
9. Add mozzarella slices
10. Add ham, spinach, and sun-dried tomatoes.
11. Add extra semolina to pizza stone and carefully slide pizza on grill.
12. Tip: Have a friend help with this step.
13. Allow to cook for 7 minutes with the lid closed.
14. Open grill and crack one egg onto the pizza.
15. Close the lid and allow to cook for 3 to 4 more minutes or until egg white is opaque.
16. Remove from grill and let rest for 5 minutes.
17. Serve and enjoy

Pepperoni Pizza

Cooking Time: 3-5 Min

Ingredients:

- Pizza Dough/Crust
- Pizza Sauce
- Mozzarella Cheese
- Pepperonis
- Other Toppings

Directions:

1. Add a layer of sauce
2. Spread your favorite toppings
3. Add an even layer of cheese
4. Add more toppings if desired
5. Heat grill to 550°F
6. Place pizza on stone
7. Cook for 3-5 minutes
8. Slice and serve!

Grilled Fathead Pizza

Ingredients:

- 10 oz Shredded Mozzarella Cheese
- 1 Egg
- 5 oz Balanced Almond Flour
- 1 tsp Pizza Seasoning
- 1/3 Cup Marinara Sauce
- 1/2 Pound Ground Italian Sausage, Ground
- 15 Pepperoni Slices
- 1 Green Bell Pepper, Chopped
- 1/2 Red Onion, Chopped
- 1 can sliced black olives
- 1 can sliced mushrooms
- 1.5 Cups Shredded Mozzarella Cheese (Topping)

Directions:

1. Preheat grill to a low temp of about 250°.
2. Melt 10 oz mozzarella cheese in microwave in 30 second increments until all melted, add 1 egg & mix. Once egg is mixed add the almond flour, baking powder & pizza seasoning.
3. Knead with hands until well incorporated (for about 3 minutes).
4. Spread dough out on a baking sheet with parchment paper.
5. Put on grill for about 5-6 minutes until crust is turning golden.
6. Then take crust off the grill, flip over & put back on parchment paper.
7. Add toppings & then put back in the grill for about 10 minutes or until desired doneness.

Pesto Burrata Grilled Pizza

Cooking Time: 3 Min

Ingredients:

- 1 Pizza Dough Ball (Store bought Dough or Homemade Dough)
- 1 Cup pesto
- 1 Cup Fresh Greens (Arugula or Spinach)
- 2 Burrata Balls
- 1/2 Cup Fresh Basil Leaves
- 4 T Olive Oil
- Salt And Pepper To Taste

Directions:

1. Fill chimney with charcoal. Place over side burner and turn flame to high, allowing charcoal to catch fire. If you do not have the side burner on your Texas Trio, you can light paper under the chimney so that it catches. We are cooking on the Akorn Jr today, so prep the base for charcoal, scrape the grates to make sure they're clean, and grab your stone or cast iron for the pizza.
2. Once coals have heated through, about 20 minutes, add them to the base of the Akorn Jr and place grates over the coals, add cast iron, and close lid to allow grill to heat up.
3. Let's prep the pizza. Cut dough ball into four equal pieces and roll each piece out to a thin circle.
4. I like to plate up all my toppings and take them out to the grill so I can make the pizzas quickly. When it's time- add a drizzle of the olive oil to the stone or cast iron and lay the dough out. Flip after about 60 seconds, once the sides start to golden and you see some bubbles forming. On the now cooked side that is up- spread ¼ cup of the pesto, add half a ball of burrata and close the lid for an additional 1-2 minutes, until the pie is cooked through. Remove from heat and top with arugula, fresh basil leaves, a drizzle of olive oil, and salt and pepper. Repeat three more times until all the pies are done. Serve hot, and enjoy!

Flat Iron Cheesy Pizza Bagels

Cooking Time: 15 Min

Ingredients:

- 3 Bagels Cut in Halves (Whatever type you prefer)
- 1 Can of Pizza Sauce
- 1 Cup of Pepperoni or Salami (Sliced)
- 2 Cups of Mozzarella Cheese
- 2 Tbsp of Butter

Directions:

1. Melt 1 Tbsp of butter on Flat Iron over Medium Heat.
2. Place bagels face down in butter and allow 2-3 minutes for them to lightly toast. Remove from heat.
3. On a separate section of the griddle, warm pepperoni/salami over medium heat for 3-4 minutes then set aside
4. On a tray or large plate, assemble bagel pizzas by spreading each with sauce, then adding desired amount of pepperoni/salami and cheese on top.
5. Place each bagel pizza back on the griddle on another Tbsp of melted butter over on medium-low heat until cheese has thoroughly melted and the bottom is toasted. (It might help to cover each bagel pizza with a basting/grill cover)
6. Serve hot.

SEAFOOD

Cedar Plank Smoked Salmon

Cooking Time: 1-1.5 Hrs

Ingredients:

- Salmon fillets
- 1/3 C. olive oil
- 1/3 C. soy sauce
- 1/3 C. maple syrup
- ½ Tsp. cayenne pepper

Directions:

1. Rinse salmon and pat dry with paper towel. 2. Mix all ingredients together and pour evenly over salmon in an airtight container. Reserve some for basting and set aside. 3. Place in refrigerator and allow to marinate for 1 hour, or longer if desired. 4. Pre-heat grill to 275°F. Soak cedar planks in water for 3 minutes before placing on the grill to warm for 5-10 minutes. 5. Place salmon on cedar planks and smoke until the internal temperature of the fish reaches 145°F, basting with reserved marinade every 30 minutes.
2. Remove from grill and serve. Enjoy!

2-burner Flat Iron Easy Shrimp Tacos

Cooking Time: 10 Min

Ingredients:

- 1 Lb. of medium-sized shrimp, deveined and peeled with tails removed
- 6-8 Flour or Corn Tortillas
- 1 Tbsp of Extra Virgin Olive Oil
- 1 Tbsp of Char-Griller Chili Lime or Taco & Fajita Rub
- 1/2 Tbsp of Garlic Powder
- 1/2 Tbsp of Onion Powder
- 1/2 Tbsp of Pepper
- A Dash of Salt
- Optional Toppings: Iceberg Lettuce, Sour Cream, Tomatoes, Cilantro, Salsa, Avocado

Directions:

1. Make these simple shrimp tacos as complex or as stuffed as you'd like. Our Rubs will take this dish to the next level, preparing it perfectly for whatever your taste buds have in mind.
2. Prep shrimp, by drying as much as possible with paper towels. In a bowl, combine shrimp with olive oil and all seasonings. With Flat Iron preheated to medium-high heat, add shrimp to cooktop and cook while occasionally stirring for about 5-6 minutes or until shrimp are no longer pink. Remove from Flat Iron. Add tortillas to the cooktop and warm up, cooking for 2-3 minutes per side. Assemble the tacos with desired toppings and serve immediately. Enjoy!

Cedar Plank Salmon

Cooking Time: 20-25 Min

Ingredients:

- Whole Coho Salmon 2 Lbs
- Cedar Plank Boards
- Olive Oil
- Kary's Roux All Purpose Seasoning
- Caribeque Lemon Garlic Seasoning
- Lemons
- Dill
- Parsley
- Asparagus (Optional)
- Garlic Parsley Butter

Directions:

1. Soak the cedar plank boards in water for one hour prior to prepping the salmon. Slice the whole salmon into four fillets, it is fine to leave the skin on. Place the salmon fillets on the cedar plank boards with a few lemon slices and asparagus.Tip: Apply olive oil directly on the cedar plank side you place the salmon to keep it from sticking.
2. Apply even coat of olive oil to the top/sides of the salmon fillets. Apply Caribeque Lemon Garlic Seasoning and Kary's Roux All Purpose Seasoning: use to taste. Add Garlic Parsley Butter to the top of each salmon: 1tsp per fillet. Add dill, parsley and additional lemons to the salmon fillets. Sprinkle parsley flakes when done to complete the prepping process.
3. Grilling directions: 20-25 minutes, internal temperature 145°
4. Preheat your grill to 400° Add cedar planks with the salmon to the grill directly over the lump Charcoal. No need to rotate, allow the grill, charcoal and cedar plank salmon to roast the salmon. Tip: It's also okay if your temperature drops: check out the recipe video on YouTube full for temperature control tips. Cook to internal temperature 145° and remove the cedar planks from the
5. Grill and it's ready for immediate eating.Tip: take the guesswork out and use the Char-Griller Grills folding probe to easily see what temperature the salon is at. Enjoy!

Grilled Coconut Lime Foil Packets

Cooking Time: 12 To 15 Min

Ingredients:

- 1 Small, Yellow Onion - Chopped
- 3 Garlic Cloves
- Shredded Sweetened Coconut - 1 Cup
- Zest and Juice from 1 Lime
- Fresh Cilantro - 1 Cup
- Extra Virgin Olive Oil - 1/4 Cup
- Soy Sauce - 1/4 Cup
- Raw Shrimp, Peeled and Deveined - 1 Pound
- Corn Kernels - 2 Cups
- 1 Zucchini - Sliced into 1/4 inch rounds and halved
- Halved Cherry Tomatoes - 1 Cup
- Salt and Pepper to Taste
- Fajita Seasoning - 1 tsp

Directions:

1. Using a blender, combine onion, garlic, coconut, lime zest, lime juice, cilantro, olive oil, and soy sauce. Blend until smooth.
2. Place marinade and shrimp in a bowl and toss to coat.
3. Set aside for 5 minutes.
4. Preheat grill to medium high heat.
5. Tear off four large squares of foil.
6. Spray one side of foil with cooking spray.
7. Divide vegetables and shrimp evenly among each packet.
8. Season with salt, pepper and fajita seasoning.
9. Foil up packets and seal completely.
10. Put packets on grill, close the lid, and grill for 6 minutes. Turn packets over and grill for 7 minutes.
11. Open packets and stir.
12. Sprinkle with fresh cilantro and serve.

Grilled Lobster Tails

Cooking Time: 10 Min

Ingredients:

- 8oz. lobster tails
- 2 sticks salted butter
- 1 Tbsp. garlic

Directions:

1. Butterfly the lobster. To do this, use a sharp knife or kitchen shears to split the lobster shell all the way to the tail. Slice the meat in half along the cut line on the shell, being careful not to slice through the lobster. Open the lobster shell-side down and lay it flat. 2. To make clarified butter, melt butter in a pan. Bring to a boil and reduce to a simmer. Skim the foam from the surface. Strain the butter to further remove residue, if desired. Add garlic and stir to combine. Pour into a small bowl and set aside to keep warm. 3. Brush lobster tails with clarified garlic butter and place on the grill, shell-side up, at 400°F for 3-4 minutes. Flip and grill for another 5-6 minutes. Lobster is done when internal temperature reaches 135°F.

Spicy Crawfish Dip

Cooking Time: 15 Min

Ingredients:

- ½ C. butter
- ½ C. chopped bell pepper
- ½ C. chopped onion (or green onion)
- 1 Tbsp. basil
- 2 cloves minced garlic
- 2 Tsp. Old bay or Cajun seasoning
- Salt and pepper, to taste
- 1 lb. pack frozen, cooked, peeled crawfish tails, thawed and undrained
- 8 oz. cream cheese, softened
- Sriracha, to taste

Directions:

1. Pre-heat grill to 350°F and add Smokin' Stone under the grates. Place a cast iron skillet on top of the grates and heat until very hot.
2. Add butter to skillet and allow to melt. Add bell pepper and onion. Sauté for 2 minutes, stirring occasionally.
3. Add basil, garlic, seasoning and salt and pepper to taste and stir. Add crawfish and stir to combine.
4. Stir in cream cheese until mixture is smooth. Stir in Sriracha sauce, to taste and allow to smoke for 10 minutes with lid closed at 350°F.
5. Remove from grill and serve with crackers or toasted French bread slices. Enjoy!

Flavor Pro Cedar Plank Salmon

Cooking Time: 25 Min

Ingredients:

- 2 Cedar Planks
- 2 Salmon Filets
- Olive Oil
- Rosemary
- Salt and Pepper to Taste

Directions:

1. Soak cedar planks in water for at least 8 hours. Set up the Flavor Pro for Indirect cooking Add 30 to 40 charcoal briquettes to one side of the flavor drawer Ignite charcoal with gas burners set to medium high Once charcoal is lit, turn off gas burners and allow to fully ash over Rub salmon on both sides with olive oil. Season with salt and pepper, rosemary sprigs and slices of lemon Place Salmon on the side of the grill away from the charcoal Cook salmon for 15 minutes or until flakey.

Grilled Salmon

Cooking Time: 20 Min

Ingredients:

- 4 Salmon Fillets
- 1/4 Cup of Olive Oil
- 2 Tbsp of Char-Griller Creole Seasoning
- 1/2 Tbsp of Garlic Powder
- 1 Tsp of Dried Parsley
- Kosher Salt
- Ground Black Pepper
- 4 Lemon Wedges

Directions:

1. Generously coat the salmon with olive oil and all seasonings. Heat your grill to medium-high heat. Add salmon fillets, flesh side down, cooking for 6-8 minutes with the grill closed. Once the meat is firm enough, flip it over, closing the lid, cooking for an additional 3-8 minutes depending on desired doneness. Remove from heat and allow the fillets to rest for 5 minutes before removing the skin and serving with lemon wedges along with any desired condiments and toppings.

Oysters "dougie-feller"

Cooking Time: 15 Min

Ingredients:

- 10-12 Large Oysters
- 2 oz. pancetta
- 2-3 Tbsp. shallot, chopped
- 2 Tbsp. unsalted butter
- 4 cloves minced garlic
- 3 Tbsp. hot pepper sauce
- 2 oz. panko crumbs
- Juice of ½ lemon
- 2 C. spinach, chopped
- Bed of rock salt

Directions:

1. Shuck oysters
2. Melt 2 Tbsp. unsalted butter in cast iron skillet
3. Sauté pancetta in skillet until crispy (5-7 minutes)
4. Add chopped shallot, and cook until fragrant, about 1 minute
5. Add 4 cloves minced garlic, cook until fragrant, about 1 minute
6. Add 3 Tbsp. hot pepper sauce, stir to incorporate
7. Mix in chopped spinach
8. Sauté until spinach begins to wilt
9. Add 2 oz of panko crumbs
10. Season with salt and pepper to taste
11. Stir in lemon juice
12. Remove from heat and set aside
13. Place 10-12 large oysters on grill at 350°F, shell side up, cooking for 5-7 minutes
14. Remove from grill and lay oysters on a bed of rock salt
15. Top oysters with pancetta and spinach mixture

Fresh Garlic Parsley Butter Salmon

Cooking Time: 30 Min

Ingredients:

- Garlic Parsley Butter
- 2 (6 oz) Salmon Mignons
- Tajin to Taste
- Dry Parsley Flakes to Taste
- Olive Oil

Directions:

1. Make Garlic Parsley Butter
2. Add Tajin seasoning to butter to taste or use favorite seafood seasoning.
3. Add 1 tbsp. of Fresh Garlic Parsley to each salmon mignons patty.
4. Add dry parsley flakes to taste.
5. Preheat your Char-griller Premium Red Kettle 14822 to 350°.
6. Insert the Char-griller Chimney in the middle of the grill in the fire pit area and do not remove it and no need to release the coals.
7. The handle will not melt inside the Premium Kettles. This will give you a hot fire in the middle of the grill for easy cast iron cooking and also raises the charcoal. The middle small grill grate can be easily moved with a Char-griller grate lifter to add charcoal.
8. Add olive oil to your cast iron skillet: just enough to coat the bottom of the skillet and place over the fire to preheat.
9. Then place the salmon on the cast iron skillet.
10. Flip Salomon after 12 minutes and toss the melted fresh garlic parsley on all sides of the salmon using a spoon.
11. Add 2 additional tbsp. to the skillet for extra flavor.
12. Then move the cast iron skillet away from the middle of the grill for a quick offset cook for 15 minutes.Tip: Continuously add the melted fresh garlic parsley on all sides of the salmon using a spoon for extra flavor.
13. Enjoy!

Honey-bourbon Glazed Salmon

Cooking Time: 45-60 Min

Ingredients:

- 1 Cedar Plank
- 1 Wild Salmon Filet
- 1 Lemon, sliced
- Lemon pepper seasoning (to taste)
- ½ C. Bourbon
- Water (enough to cover the cedar plank)
- 3 Tbsp. Honey
- 1 oz. Bourbon
- 1 Tsp. Lemon Zest

Directions:

1. Remove the pin bones from the salmon filet with fish bone tweezers. Pour water and bourbon into a large baking dish and soak cedar plank for a minimum of 1 hour.
2. Place salmon filet on cedar plank, sprinkle with lemon pepper seasoning, to taste, and cover with sliced lemons.
3. Prepare the grill for offset smoking by adding citrus wood chunks to the Side Fire Box. Place the salmon on the grill and smoke at 250° - 275°F for approximately 45 - 60 minutes.
4. Mix the honey, bourbon and lemon zest together in a bowl to make the glaze. After 30 minutes, intermittently brush the honey/bourbon glaze on the salmon.
5. Enjoy the deliciousness!

Gravity 980 Grilled Lobster Tails

Cooking Time: 10 Min

Ingredients:

- 6 Lobster Tails
- 1/3 Cup of Melted Butter
- 1 Tbsp OF Extra Virgin Olive Oil
- 1 Lemon
- 1 Tbsp of Parsley
- 1 Tbsp of Chives
- 1 Tbsp of Minced Garlic
- 1 Tbsp of Char-Griller Creole Rub
- 1/2 Tsp of Salt
- 1/2 Tsp of Pepper

Directions:

1. To prep lobster tails, using kitchen shears, cut the top of the shell lengthwise down the middle. Using a sharp knife, cut through this slit, halfway through the flesh, excluding the very tip of the tail. Flatten each tail so the shell opens around the meat. Place a skewer through each tail to prevent it from curling during cooking. In a bowl, combine butter, parsley, ½ the chives, minced garlic and Creole rub. Line tails on a baking sheet and brush each lightly with oil, salt and pepper. Remove the fire shutter from your Gravity 980, load and light the hopper then set to 350°F. Place the lobster tails, flesh side down on the grill and allow to cook for 5 minutes. Flip each tail over and drizzle the tops generously with garlic butter mixture. Grill for additional 5 minutes or until lobster becomes fully cooked. Sprinkle finished lobster tails with remaining chives and serve with lemon wedges. Enjoy!

Grilled Seafood Boil

Cooking Time: 20-25 Min

Ingredients:

- 2 Lb. Of Large Shrimp, Deveined and Peeled, Remove the tails during prep if you prefer
- 2 Andouille Sausages (Thinly Sliced)
- 2 Large Ears Of Corn, Shucked and Each Cut Into 4 Small Cobs
- 1 Lb. of Red Bliss potatoes (Cut Into Small Cubes)
- 1 Lemon (Sliced Into 4 Wedges)
- 4 Tbsp of Butter
- 4 Tsp of Char-Griller "Creole" Rub
- 4 Tsp Of Italian Seasoning
- 4 Tsp Of Minced Garlic
- Extra Virgin Olive Oil
- Salt and Pepper To Taste

Directions:

1. Preheat your grill to medium-high heat. Arrange 4 pieces of aluminum foil, about 1 foot long for each packet. Evenly divide shrimp, sausages, corn, potatoes and lemon amongst each "packet". Drizzle each packet with olive oil, 1 tsp of garlic, salt and pepper, and 1 tsp of Char-Griller's Creole seasoning. Use hands to mix to ensure all elements are coated evenly. Top each off packet with 1 tsp of Italian Seasoning, and 1 Tbsp of butter. Fold each packet, ensuring the entire mixture is covered and twist the edges seal it closed. Place the foil packets directly on the grill and cook for 20-25 minutes or until they are cooked to your liking. Serve warm, enjoy!

Fish And Chips

Cooking Time: 12 Min

Ingredients:

- 4 cod filets
- 3-4 Idaho potatoes
- 1 C. flour
- 1 C. milk
- 1 egg
- 1 Tsp. Old Bay seasoning

Directions:

1. Heat grill to 350-400°F.
2. Let oil heat up in skillet until it sizzles when splashed with a few drops of water.
3. 3-4 Idaho potatoes with skin on, cut into french fries.
4. Let them soak in water for 20-30 minutes to remove excess starch.
5. Pat dry on paper towels before frying.
6. Fries are done when they begin to turn golden
7. Mix batter until only a few clumps of flour remain. Don't over mix.
8. Dredge fish in flour seasoned in Old Bay, if you prefer, before dipping in batter
9. Let fish filets fry on each side for 2-3 minutes, until golden crispy brown.
10. Serve with coleslaw and tartar sauce. Delicious!

Buffalo Lemon Shrimp

Cooking Time: 12 Min

Ingredients:

- Raw Shrimp, Peeled and Deveined - 1 Pound
- Hot Sauce (I Use Buffalo Sauce for this Recipe) - 3 Tablespoons
- Minced Garlic - 1 Tablespoon
- Olive Oil - 2 Tablespoons
- Juiced Lemon - 1
- Lemon Cut Into Wedges for Serving - 1
- Salt to Taste

Directions:

1. Taking advantage of seasonal ingredients is the name of the game, so for the remainder of the summer, chicken wings are going to have to move aside. If you haven't been grilling shrimp this season, now is the time. She loves to use charcoal for this recipe, as shrimp cook quickly and charcoal flame provides so much flavor in such a short amount of time. Let's dig in!
2. Light your charcoal in your chimney and wait until the bricks are glowing red and ashy around the edges. Dump under the grates of your Char-Griller Grill, and close the lid, letting the grates heat for 5-10 minutes.
3. While grill is heating, toss shrimp with buffalo sauce, minced garlic, the juice of one lemon, olive oil, and plenty of salt. Let marinate on the counter for a few minutes.
4. Once the grill is heated, spray the grates with non-stick spray, and lay your shrimp and lemon wedges out to cook. Grill on each side for 2 minutes, until some deep char marks form, and they are curled up and a beautiful vibrant pink color.
5. Serve on a large tray with grilled lemon wedges and an extra sprinkle of salt! These are super delicious on a salad, in a taco, or as the main dish at your next barbecue! Happy Grilling.

Shrimp 'n Grits

Cooking Time: 20-25 Min

Ingredients:

- 1 lb. shrimp, peeled and deveined
- Original All-Purpose BBQ rub, to taste, or preferred rub
- ½ red bell pepper, chopped
- ½ onion, chopped
- Handful of cilantro, chopped
- 4 C. water
- 1 Tsp. salt
- 1 C. stone-ground grits
- 2-3 Tbsp. butter
- 4 oz. heavy cream
- 2 oz. Parmesan cheese
- Salt and pepper, to taste

Directions:

1. Pre-heat grill to 375°F. Bring water to a boil, add grits and cook until water is absorbed, about 20-25 minutes. Remove from heat, stir in butter, cheese and heavy cream. Add salt and pepper, to taste and stir. Set aside. 2. While grits are cooking, melt butter in skillet and sauté red pepper and onions until soft, about 5-7 minutes, stirring occasionally. 3. Add shrimp and season with Original All-Purpose BBQ Rub and cook for 3-5 minutes, until opaque and fully cooked. Add cilantro and salt and pepper, to taste and stir to combine.

2. To serve, spoon grits into bowls and top with shrimp and red pepper mixture. Garnish with more cilantro and enjoy!

BEEF

Gravity 980 Brisket

Cooking Time: 8 Hrs

Ingredients:

- 1 Whole Brisket (Flat And Point) Trimmed
- 1/4 Cup of Extra Virgin Olive Oil
- Kosher Salt
- Freshly Ground Black Pepper
- Garlic Powder (Optional)

Directions:

1. Remove your brisket from the refrigerator, pat it dry and allow it to sit out for 30 minutes to an hour. In a small bowl, combine your seasonings then thoroughly coat the exterior of the brisket with olive oil. Remove fire shutter from the Gravity 980, load the hopper, then preheat it to 225-250°F. Season the exterior of your brisket thoroughly with the seasoning mixture. Close the lid and allow it to smoke for 7-8 hours without opening the lid. After this point, you may optionally remove it from the smoker and wrap it in butcher paper or aluminum foil before returning it to the smoker. Cook until the brisket's internal temperature has reached around 200-205°F and a nice dark bark has formed. Remove it from the smoker and allow it to rest 1 hour in the butcher paper or on a cutting board before slicing. Be sure to slice against the grain. Enjoy!

Pastrami Swiss Burger

Cooking Time: 40 Min

Ingredients:

- 2 lbs. ground beef
- ½ lb. Pastrami, sliced
- 2 eggs, beaten
- Steak BBQ rub
- 1 C. beef all-purpose sauce
- Swiss cheese, sliced
- Hamburger buns
- Condiments of choice

Directions:

1. Place ground beef in large bowl, add eggs and season with Steak BBQ rub, or your favorite rub, to taste and sauce. Mix ingredients by hand until just blended.
2. Form 1" thick patties and place on a wax paper lined tray. Place tray with patties in refrigerator and allow to chill for 10-15 minutes.
3. Place chilled patties on the grill at 350°F for 5 minutes per side, with a quarter turn halfway through for good sear marks.
4. Bush burgers with more sauce, if desired and top with sliced pastrami and cheese. Allow cheese to melt, about 1-2 minutes. Burgers are done when internal temperature reaches 165°F for medium-rare.

Flavor Pro Italian Sausage Burgers

Cooking Time: 15 Min

Ingredients:

- 2 Tbsp Canola Oil
- 1 Large Green Bell Pepper, Sliced Thin
- 1 Large Red Bell Pepper, Sliced Thin
- 1 Large Yellow Bell Pepper, Sliced Thin
- 1/2 Large Sweet Onion, Sliced Thin
- 1 Pound Sweet Italian Sausage Meat
- 1/3 Cup Panko Bread Crumbs
- 1 Large Egg
- 2 Tbsp Italian Seasoning
- 1 Tbsp Chili Powder
- 2 Tbsp Hot Sauce (Optional)
- 1 tsp Salt
- 1 tsp Pepper
- 8 Slices Provolone Cheese
- 4 Italian Sandwich Rolls

Directions:

1. Prepare Flavor Pro for direct heat (medium-high, 350-400°F) For best results, fill all three zones of the Flavor Drawer with charcoal. Light coals using all four gas burners on high. Be sure grill lid is open before you ignite the burners. Keep both smoke stacks open.
2. Heat the oil in a large cast iron skillet on the grill.
3. Add peppers and onions to oil. Cook with grill lid on, for 6-10 minutes, flipping occasionally. Look for peppers to be tender and onions to be translucent and browning on edges. Pull off and set aside.
4. In a large mixing bowl, add sausage, bread crumbs, egg, and seasonings. Combine well with hands.
5. Form into 4 evenly sized patties.
6. Ensure grill is still hot and add more coals if necessary.
7. Cook sausage burger patties 4-5 minutes per side until cooked through. Look for an internal temperature of 150°-160°F.
8. Remove from heat. Add 2 slices of provolone cheese immediately to each burger. Place on the Italian sandwich rolls and top with peppers and onions. Add your favorite condiments. Yellow mustard and hot sauce makes for great additions!
9. Enjoy!

Chili In A Bread Bowl

Ingredients:

- 2 Lbs Ground Beef
- 8 Hot Link Sausages
- 8 Hot Italian Sausage
- 5 McCormick Mild Chili Seasoning Packets
- 2 Red Onions
- 1 Red Bell Pepper
- 1 Green Bell Pepper
- 2 Jalapenos
- 4 Garlic Cloves
- 4 10oz Cans of Diced Tomatoes and Green Chilies
- 2 Cans Pinto Beans
- 2 Cans Red Kidney Beans
- Shredded Cheese
- Bread Loaf (Bread Bowls)

Directions:

1. Chop your green pepper, red pepper, and red onion Using the Side Burner on our Triple Play, cook ground beef with diced garlic and jalapenos in a large pot Once the beef is cooked, add the 4 cans of diced tomatoes and green chilies Add the 4 cans of beans and mix to combine Add the 5 McCormick seasoning packets Now that your sausages are charred, slice them all and add to the pot Simmer for 30-45 minutes Hollow out your bread loaf with a paring knife to create the bowls Serve in the bread bowls and top with shredded cheese and raw red onions (or whatever else you like!)
2. Pitt Tips: Spice it up a little more by adding your favorite hot sauce, we like Tapatio! Add even more flavor by adding in your favorite beer!

Peppered Sirloin With Bacon-mushroom Sauce

Cooking Time: 2 Hrs

Ingredients:

- 12 oz. sirloin steaks, 1-1½" thick
- ½ lb. baby Portabella mushrooms, sliced
- ½ lb. peppered bacon, chopped
- 2 C. beef stock
- 2 Tbsp. all-purpose flour
- 2 Tbsp. minced garlic
- 2 Tsp. Steak BBQ rub

Directions:

1. Fry bacon in batches, if needed, in a pan to desired crispness according to package directions, drain grease and chop when cool. Set aside in a medium bowl. Do not wipe pan. 2. Add mushrooms to the same pan and sauté until tender, 5-7 minutes. Add to bowl with bacon and mix well. Do not wipe pan. 3. Add flour to pan from bacon and mushrooms and whisk into bacon grease. Add garlic and sauté 30-45 seconds, until fragrant. Slowly pour in beef broth and stir continuously to thicken sauce. 4. Add in mushrooms and bacon and stir to incorporate. 5. Transfer all ingredients to cast iron skillet with beans and mix well. 6. Remove pan from heat and set aside.
2. Sirloin
3. Rinse sirloin and pat dry with paper towel. Season sirloin generously on both sides with Steak BBQ rub, or your favorite rub and let rest until meat reaches room temperature. 2. Place sirloin directly on the grill at 400°F for 12 minutes per side, rotating a quarter turn halfway through for good sear marks on each side. Meat is done when internal temperature reaches 140°F for medium-rare. Remove sirloin from grill and allow to rest for 8-10 minutes before slicing.
4. Serve with bacon-mushroom sauce and enjoy!

Italian Burgers

Cooking Time: 20 Min

Ingredients:

- Italian Sausage - 1/2 Pound
- Ground Beef - 1/2 Pound
- Portabella Mushroom Caps, Gills Removed - 5
- Ciabatta Rolls, Sliced Lengthwise - 4
- Shredded Parmesan - 1/3 Cup
- Diced Green Peppers - 1/2 Cup
- Crushed Red Pepper - 1/2 Teaspoon
- Bacon - 24 slices
- Prepared Marinara - 1/2 Cup
- Munster Cheese - 4 Slices
- Ball of Mozzarella Sliced into 1/4" Slices
- Italian Seasoning - 1/2 Teaspoon
- Whisked Egg- 1
- Oil for Frying

Directions:

1. Light charcoal and push to one side of the grill, leveling them out to one layer
2. Pour 1" of oil in pan and place directly over coals and heat to 350F
3. Place flour, salt, and Italian seasoning in a shallow bowl and dip each slice of cheese in the flour mixture, coating each side
4. Dip each slice into egg
5. Fully coat each slice in egg, then back again in the flour mixture. Allow to set, refrigerated for 15 minutes.
6. Meanwhile, dice one portabella cap 7. Mix both meats, diced mushrooms, bell pepper, red pepper, and parmesan together just until combined
7. Spoon meat mixture into each portabella cap
8. Wrap each burger patty with bacon. I found it easiest to weave 6 pieces of bacon, lay the patty in the middle and wrap the weaved bacon carefully around
9. Place patties on the side of the grill with no charcoal, flip patties half way through
10. While patties are cooking, fry the mozzarella until golden brown on each side and place on paper towel to drain
11. Cook burgers until bacon is crispy and internal temperature is 140F
12. Place cheese slices on top of each burger. Remove from grill when internal temperature reaches 145F
13. Add patties to bottom bun, top with fried mozzarella and marinara sauce

Korean Style Beef Short Ribs

Ingredients:

- 4-6 Lbs Beef Short Ribs
- 2 Tbsp Minced Garlic
- 1/2 Cup Brown Sugar
- 1 Cup Soy Sauce

Directions:

1. Mix soy sauce, brown sugar, and minced garlic. Add beef short ribs and marinate for at least 4 hrs. Preheat grill to 450F. Grill direct over coals for 3-4 minutes per side. Garnish with sliced green onions if desired, enjoy!

Cold Weather Chili

Cooking Time: 30 Min

Ingredients:

- 2-3 Tbsp. butter
- 1 lb. ground beef
- 1 medium white onion, chopped
- ½ green pepper, chopped
- ½ red pepper, chopped
- 14.5 oz can pinto beans, drained
- Your favorite chili powder or pre-made chili seasoning
- One small can tomato paste
- 1 can of your favorite beer (optional) or 1½ C. beef broth
- Salt and pepper, to taste

Directions:

1. Preheat grill to 350°F. Melt butter in a large cast iron pot.
2. Add chopped onion, peppers, ground beef and pinto beans and cook for 5 minutes, covered.
3. After 5 minutes, uncover and add chili powder or seasoning. Mix well, cover and cook for 10 minutes until meat is browned.
4. Add chili paste and/or tomato paste and beer (optional, or use beef broth) and stir. Cook 15 minutes to reduce and heat through. Add salt and pepper to taste and add water if needed.
5. Serve with your favorite chili fixings! Enjoy!

The All American Burger

Cooking Time: 6 Min

Ingredients:

- 80/20 Ground Chuck- 1 Pound
- Steak- 8 ounces
- Salt
- Pepper
- Fire

Directions:

1. Cube your steak and grind together with coarse plate in the grinder.
2. Once fully ground, change the plate to a finer grind, and grind again. This will help the fat and meat combine well so that the burgers stay together.
3. Once ground, form the patties, about 4 inches.
4. Create a well in the center of the patties to help with even cooking.
5. Put the burgers in the fridge for up to 1 hour after forming the patties.
6. Fire up the grill and bring up to 400F
7. Season the patties with fresh ground black pepper and fresh ground sea salt.
8. Cook the burgers for about 4-6 minutes. Close the lid while doing this.
9. Flip once, and let cook.
10. Add cheese to the burgers and let the cheese melt over the patties.
11. Toast the bun on the grill to prevent a soggy bun when the juices of the burger comes out.
12. Once done, assemble your burger as you like and show your friends and family how you have become a true #grillionaire and that you are the KING of the cul de sac.

Smoked Bacon Wrapped Cheese Stuffed Avocado

Cooking Time: 1.5-2 Hrs

Ingredients:

- 2 avocados
- 1 lb. ground beef
- 1 lb. bacon
- 1 C. shredded cheese
- ¼ C. Original All-Purpose BBQ rub
- BBQ Sauce

Directions:

1. Split, peel and pit avocado
2. Make 2 cheese balls the size of removed avocado pit
3. Put cheese ball in seed hole
4. Add rub on each side of avocado, then close avocados
5. Use half of the ground beef for each avocado and wrap avocados until fully covered
6. Season ground beef generously with Original All-Purpose BBQ Rub, or your favorite rub, to taste.
7. Wrap bacon around the beef (4-5 strips per avocado)
8. Season bacon with rub
9. Cook for 1 1/2 - 2 hours at 250°F
10. Baste with BBQ sauce and cook for additional 15 minutes

Breakfast Burritos On The Flat Iron

Ingredients:

- Pack of 8 Breakfast Sausage Circles
- Pack of Shredded Cheese
- Burrito Tortillas (Large)
- Pack of Thick-Cut Bacon
- Dozen Eggs
- Package of Diced Frozen Hash Browns

Directions:

1. Perfect for taking on the go or preparing for the family to add some pizzazz into your mornings, these Breakfast Burritos are easy to assemble and allow you to choose toppings to make it your own.
2. Start with the hash browns on high-med/high heat with some oil. Keep an eye on them. Throw on the sausage and bacon. Cut up the sausage for the burritos. Once everything is cooked, move off to the side Warm-up a burrito to make easier to fold Ladle some eggs on to the griddle Add cheese and other toppings Remove burrito wrap Fold the egg into an omelet place on burrito wrap and fold Enjoy!

Saucy Brisket Burnt Ends

Cooking Time: 6-7 Hrs

Ingredients:

- 6 Pound Brisket Flat or Point.
- Original Sin Mustard for Binder
- Beef Rub
- 50/50 Salt & Pepper Blend

Directions:

1. Prepping
2. Trim brisket with sharp knife on a cutting board then place on a tray to apply binder and seasonings.
3. Apply mustard to all sides of the brisket as a binder for the seasonings.
4. Apply seasonings to all sides of the brisket.
5. Smoking
6. Add Char-Griller Drip Pan with water underneath the grill grate of your smoker/grill. This will add moisture to the brisket during the long smoke and also the meat drippings and juice from the spritz will fall in there for less of a mess.
7. Preheat your smoker/grill to 240°-250°: going low n' slow at this temperature is key for brisket. 1 Hour Per Pound.
8. Add Brisket to smoker/grill on to a cardboard with butcher paper. Using the Cardboard with butcher paper in the shape of the brisket is a great method that keeps the bottom of the brisket from drying out & allows you to easily move the brisket around in the smoker/grill from side to side. It will keep the brisket juicy and moist.
9. Tip: Place the brisket fat side up.
10. Spritz every hour with apple juice and rotate brisket from left to right for even smoking. Remember the brisket is on the cardboard and it's really easy to rotate without having to touch the meat. Spritzing with Apple juice helps keep the brisket moist during the long smoke, adds flavor and helps create the black bark we are looking for.
11. Maintaining your fire is key, check on your fire roughly every hour and add charcoal/wood as needed. Try to avoid your smoker from exceeding 250° and getting under 240°. Brisket is meant for low n' slow at about 240°-250° and keeping your fire steady throughout the cook is important.
12. Remove brisket from the smoker when it reaches 160°, discard the cardboard & butcher paper. Place the brisket in a pan with apple juice, water & beef rub then cover with foil.

13. Tip: Take the guesswork out and use the Char-griller Grills Remote Thermometer & Folding Probe Thermometer to easily see what temperature the meat is at.
14. Add brisket back to the smoker until temperature 199°-200° has been reached. Tip: no need to waste your smoking wood when the brisket is wrapped. Use only the charcoal as your fuel at temperature 240°-250° until the brisket is done.
15. Remove brisket onto a cutting board and slice into cubes. Then add the the brisket cubes back to the pan with the brisket juices with Blues Hog Raspberry Chipotle Sauce. Get them sauced up and place back in the smoker/grill uncovered for an additional 30 minutes.
16. When you remove from the smoker/grill allow to rest for 5-10 minutes and enjoy!

Smoked Baked Spaghetti

Cooking Time: 1 Hrs

Ingredients:

- 1 lb. ground beef
- 1 lb. spaghetti
- 2 Tbsp. melted butter
- 1 C. onion, diced
- 1-2 cloves garlic, minced
- 1 chopped green pepper, cored and seeded
- 1½ C. spaghetti sauce
- 2 C. grated or shredded cheese (Colby jack, Mozzarella or Parmesan)
- 2 C. mushrooms, sliced (optional)
- 2.25 oz. can of black olives, drained (optional)
- 1 Tsp. salt
- 1 Tsp. pepper

Directions:

1. Fill stockpot with water and salt and bring to a boil. 2. Cook spaghetti until al dente, following directions on package. Drain and set aside in a large bowl. 3. Sauté onion, green pepper and mushrooms in a large skillet until tender, about 5-7 minutes. Set aside in a small bowl. Do not wipe pan. 4. Brown ground beef in the same pan and add minced garlic, salt and pepper and stir. 5. Drain grease from ground beef and add green pepper, onion, mushrooms and spaghetti sauce. Mix well. 6. Add 2 Tbsp. melted butter and ½ cup of grated cheese to cooked spaghetti and stir. 7. Place 1/3 of meat sauce in the bottom of a well-greased 9 x 13 baking pan. 8. Layer 1/3 of cheese on top of meat sauce. 9. Add all of the spaghetti and spread evenly. 10. Pour the rest of the meat sauce on top of spaghetti in an even layer. 1 Bake for 45 minutes at 350°F. 12. Spread the remaining cheese and add black olives in an even layer across the top. 13. Bake at 350°F for an additional 10-15 minutes until cheese is melted.
2. Let cool for 10 minutes, then serve!
3. Note: The mushrooms and black olives in this recipe can be swapped out with toppings of your choice.

Smoked Meatloaf

Cooking Time: 2 Hrs

Ingredients:

- 2 Lbs. Ground Beef
- 1/2 Cup of Onion (Minced)
- 1/4 Cup of Garlic (Minced)
- 2 Eggs (Cracked)
- 1 Tsp of Salt
- 1 Tsp of Pepper
- 1 Tsp of Cayenne Pepper
- 3/4 Cup of Bread Crumbs
- 1 Tbsp of Worcestershire Sauce
- 1/2 Cup of Ketchup
- 1/4 Cup of Brown Sugar
- 1 Tbsp Yellow or Dijon Mustard
- 1 Tbsp of BBQ Sauce

Directions:

1. Preheat your smoker to 225-250°F. In a large mixing bowl, combine all of the ingredients(1-9) for the loaf, thoroughly kneading together. Form into desired load shape. Place the meatloaf into the smoker and smoke for 2 hours or until the internal temperature reaches 160°F. Allow to rest for 30 minutes before slicing. Combine the ingredients(10-13) for the sauce thoroughly and apply to the top of the meatloaf once it has begun to cool down. Serve warm. Enjoy!

Leftover Brisket Nachos

Cooking Time: 20 Min

Ingredients:

- Tortilla Chips
- Leftover Brisket
- Shredded Cheddar and Monterey Jack Cheese
- Heavy Cream
- Canned Diced Chilis
- Sour Cream
- Limes
- Pickled Jalapenos
- Black Beans
- Avocados
- Radish
- Pico De Gallo: Tomatoes, Onion, Jalapeno, Cilantro

Directions:

1. Prepare your pico de gallo and guacamole
2. Combine diced tomato, jalapeno, onion and cilantro in a bowl and mix with salt and pepper and lime juice
3. Mash 2 avocados together and combine with ½ cup of the pico for some easy guacamole
4. In a skillet prepare the cheese sauce by adding 3 cups shredded cheese and 2 cans of diced chilis. Slowly mix in ½ cup heavy cream and stir until smooth
5. Reheat your leftover brisket in another skillet
6. On a large cookie sheet begin layering your nachos
7. Chips, brisket, black beans, cheese sauce, more chips, brisket, beans cheese sauce.
8. ALWAYS double layer the nachos when possible
9. Top with pico de gallo, pickled jalapenos, sour cream, and guacamole!
10. Garnish with radish and lime wedges and enjoy!

Smoked Brisket

Cooking Time: 10 Hrs

Ingredients:

- 10 ½ lb. beef brisket
- ½ C. paprika
- ¼ C. packed light brown sugar
- 3 Tbsp. salt
- 3 Tbsp. coarse black pepper
- 3 Tbsp. Chili powder
- Apple juice
- Water

Directions:

1. Using a sharp knife, trim the fat from the brisket leaving an even, thin layer on the top. 2. In a medium bowl, combine paprika, light brown sugar, Chili powder, salt and pepper and mix well to make rub seasoning. Using your hands, or a shaker, generously apply rub all over. 3. Wrap the brisket in plastic wrap and refrigerate for at least 12 hours. 4. When setting up the grill, add wood chips/chunks to charcoal and add Smokin' Stone with an aluminum pan on top. Pour apple juice and water into pan, about halfway full. Place a temperature probe at grate level and heat grill to 220°F. 5. Place brisket on grates, fat side up, and allow to smoke for 5 hours. After 5 hours, wrap brisket in butcher paper and return to grill at 220°F. Brisket is done when internal temperature reaches 195°F. Allow brisket to rest for 1 hour.
2. Slice, serve and enjoy!

PORK

Flavor Pro Quick And Easy Grilled Pork Tenderloin

Ingredients:

- 2 Pork Tenderloin
- 2 tsp Paprika
- 1 tsp Garlic Powder
- 1 tsp Cilantro
- 1 tsp Oregano
- Salt and Pepper to Taste
- Olive Oil

Directions:

1. Blend spices together in a bowl. Rub pork with olive oil and then season liberally on both sides with spice blend.
2. Set up the Flavor Pro for direct cooking. Ignite burners and turn to medium high.
3. Place pork on the grill and cook for 8 to 10 minutes per side or until the internal temperature reads 165 degrees.
4. Remove from grill and let rest for 10 minutes.

Brown Sugar Glazed Smoked Ham

Cooking Time: 2 Hrs

Ingredients:

- 11 lb. ham
- 1 C. brown sugar
- 1 C. brown mustard, or preferred

Directions:

1. Combine brown sugar and mustard together in a small bowl to make glaze. Mix well.
2. Score ham in a diamond pattern and generously brush on glaze.
3. Place glazed ham in large baking dish or cast-iron skillet onto the grill to smoke at 325°F for 2 hours. Ham is done when internal temperature reaches 140°F.
4. Remove ham from grill and let rest for 10 minutes before slicing and serving.

Flat Iron Griddle Breakfast Sandwich

Cooking Time: 5 Min

Ingredients:

- 2 Cups Of Kodiak Cakes Pancake And Waffle Mix
- 2 Cups Of Water
- 6 Eggs
- Egg Rings
- Syrup
- 1 Pack Of Bacon

Directions:

1. Mix pancake and waffle mix with water until the mix is no longer lumpy. Place egg rings on griddle and pour pancake batter into the egg rings , add a little swirl of syrup while batter is cooking. Once the batter has a nice bubble to it remove the egg ring and flip the griddle cake. Scramble or fry your eggs and cook the bacon , construct sandwich and enjoy

Pork Belly Burnt Ends On The Akorn

Cooking Time: 2 Hrs

Ingredients:

- Slab of Pork Belly
- BBQ Rub
- 1 Stick Butter
- 1/2 Cup Brown Sugar
- Honey
- BBQ sauce
- 8 oz Apple Juice

Directions:

1. Remove skin from pork belly Cut up pork belly in 5" squares Set smoker to 250-275F - indirect - add cherry wood Place cubed pork belly pieces on smoker - cook for 1.5-2 hours Place pork belly in aluminum pan - pour in brown sugar, honey and pads of your butter Cover, and place in smoker for another 1.5-2hrs (until about 205F) Grab a new pan.. drizzle with glaze(4 oz apple juice 1 cup of bbq sauce) and shake up so they're covered Return pieces to smoker, uncovered for approx 5-10 mins until tacky Enjoy!

Ultimate Pork Belly Sliders

Cooking Time: 2:15 Hrs

Ingredients:

- 4 lb. pork belly
- Yellow mustard
- Original All-Purpose BBQ rub, to taste
- Your favorite sweet BBQ rub, to taste
- Hawaiian sweet rolls or your favorite roll for sliders
- Your favorite toppings
- Your favorite BBQ sauce

Directions:

1. Remove the skin from the pork belly and season the top generously with a layer of yellow mustard, followed by Original All-Purpose BBQ rub and your favorite sweet BBQ sauce, to taste.
2. Pre-heat grill to 275°F for indirect heat with a Smokin' Stone. Allow the belly to smoke for 2 hours or until internal temperature reaches 175°F. Remove the belly from the grill and allow to rest.
3. After removing the pork belly and Smokin' Stone, stir the charcoal and open up both vents to allow the grill to reach maximum temperature for searing.
4. While the grill is heating up, slice the pork belly into ¼" thick strips and arrange on the grill. Work in batches if needed. Fry the belly for 3 minutes on each side, to allow the fat to render. Season the belly with BBQ rub again, if desired.
5. Slice the pack of Hawaiian sweet rolls in half and arrange the pork belly on the bottom half. Cover with the top half and brush with melted butter and garlic, if desired. Place the rolls in a large pan and back onto the grill to crisp up for 10 minutes.
6. Remove the pan from the grill and allow the rolls to cool slightly before slicing into individual sliders. Add your favorite toppings and sauce and enjoy!

Baby Back Ribs

Cooking Time: 3 Hrs

Ingredients:

- Salt
- Pepper
- Brown Sugar
- Garlic Salt
- Onion Salt
- Paprika

Directions:

1. Mix everything together and rub on ribs
2. Cover the ribs with foil and refrigerate overnight
3. Grill on 250° for 3 hours and take off
4. Throw your favorite BBQ sauce on and refold and grill till the BBQ sauce caramelizes. Take off and enjoy!

Quick And Easy Grilled Pork Tenderloin

Cooking Time: 25 Min

Ingredients:

- 1 Pork Tenderloin
- 1 Tsp Paprika
- 1/2 Tsp Garlic Powder
- 1/2 Tsp Cilantro
- 1/2 Tsp Oregano
- Salt and Pepper to Taste
- Olive Oil

Directions:

1. Blend spices together in a bowl. Rub pork with olive oil and then season liberally on both sides with spice blend. Set up the Flavor Pro™ for direct cooking. Ignite burners and turn to medium high. Place pork on the grill and cook for 8 to 10 minutes per side or until the internal temperature reads 165 degrees. Remove from grill and let rest for 10 minutes.

Flavor Pro Smoked Pork Shoulder

Cooking Time: 90 Minutes Per Pound And Then 1 Hour Rest Hrs

Ingredients:

- 5 to 6 Pound Bone-In Pork Shoulder or Boston Butt
- Char-Griller Rib Rub
- Spray Bottle Full of Apple Juice and Oil

Directions:

1. Trim excess fat from the pork shoulder. (Skip this step if it is Boston Butt.) Score the remaining fat with a sharp knife.
2. Rub a liberal amount of Rib Spice Rub on the pork. Make sure each side is evenly coated.
3. Place pork in the fridge for at least 12 hours.
4. Remove pork from fridge one hour before placing on the grill.
5. Cover the left-most and center Wood Product Zones of the Flavor Drawer with foil to catch the grease.
6. Place 15 to 20 charcoal briquettes in the far right side of the Flavor Drawer.
7. Turn the burners on high and ignite. Allow the briquettes to fully ash over.
8. Once the briquettes have ashed over, add two to three wood chunks to the charcoal.
9. To Use a Log: Place a log of no more than 3 inches in diameter and 7 inches long the right-most wood product zone. Light using the right most burner.
10. The log should take about 5 to 6 minutes to ignite.
11. After the log has ignited, turn off the gas burner and allow the grill to preheat.
12. Using a Grilling Glove, adjust the smokestacks until the internal temperature of the pit holds steady at 225.
13. Place the pork over the foil and close the grill.
14. Baste pork with Apple juice every 30 to 60 minutes.
15. Make sure to keep an eye on the pit temperature. Add another log every hour or so.
16. Smoke until internal temperature is 195 to 210 degrees Fahrenheit and remove from grill.
17. Tip: If your pork shoulder hits the dreaded "stall" (won't get above 165 degrees Fahrenheit or starts dropping, wrap it in foil, add some apple juice and place back on the grill. This will get it going again.
18. Allow pork to rest for 30 minutes to an hour for best results.

Asian Pork Belly Skewers

Cooking Time: 2 Hrs

Ingredients:

- Pork Belly Cut into 1 1/2" Cubes - 2 Pounds
- Pineapple Cut into 1 1/2" Cubes - 1
- Char-Griller Rib Rub
- Skewers Soaked in Water
- Chopped Green Onions and Sesame Seeds - For Garnish
- Chili Garlic Sauce - 1 Tablespoon
- Rice Wine Vinegar - 1 Teaspoon
- Chopped Garlic - 1 Teaspoon
- Orange Zest - 1 Teaspoon
- Soy Sauce - 2 Teaspoons

Directions:

1. Light grill for indirect heat
2. In a large bowl, toss pork belly with rub until generously coated
3. Skewer pineapple and pork belly, alternating between the two
4. Please skewers on the grill
5. Rotate skewers after an hour
6. Meanwhile, place all sauce ingredients in a small sauce pan
7. Chili Garlic Sauce Rice Wine Vinegar Chopped Garlic Range Zest Soy Sauce Honey Ground Ginger
8. Bring the sauce to a simmer and allow to cook until thickened. Approximately 15 minutes
9. Allow to cool
10. After two hours, brush the skewers with sauce. Allow the sauce to set for approximately 30 minutes
11. When ready to serve, sprinkle with sesame seeds and green onions

Pork Tenderloin Sliders

Cooking Time: 8-10 Min

Ingredients:

- (2) 1 lb. pork tenderloins
- Salt and pepper, to taste
- Olive oil, for brushing
- Slider buns

Directions:

1. Pre-heat grill to 400°F. Rinse tenderloins and pat dry with paper towel. 2. Generously season with salt and pepper or use Original All-Purpose BBQ rub, to taste. 3. Place pork tenderloins on the grill at 400°F for 4 minutes per side, brushing with olive oil occasionally, and turning to ensure good sear marks on each side. Pork is done when internal temperature reaches 140°F. 4. Toast slider buns for 1-2 minutes before serving.
2. Brush with a layer of BBQ sauce and allow pork to rest for 10 minutes before slicing and serving on toasted slider buns.

Blueberry Pork Belly Burnt Ends

Cooking Time: 3.5 Hrs

Ingredients:

- Pork Belly - 2 lbs
- Char-Griller Rib Rub
- Butter - 1/2 stick
- Fresh Blueberries - 2 Cups
- Apple Juice - 1/4 Cup
- Sugar - 1/4 Cup
- Cornstarch - 1 Tbs
- Lemon Juice - 1 Tbs
- Cayenne - 1 tsp (optional)

Directions:

1. Cut the pork belly into 1-1 ½ inch cubes.
2. Season the cubes liberally on all sides.
3. Prepare the fire to get the smoker up to 275 F.
4. Tip: Put the pork belly into the freezer 20-30 minutes before you cube. This will help with the cutting process.
5. Once the smoker has reached 275 F put the pork belly onto the grill with the fat side facing down.
6. Spritz every 40-45 minutes until the pork belly starts to read an internal temp of 190 F.
7. Place the cubes in an aluminum pan and add one cup of the blueberry sauce and the butter. Toss the cubes to make sure the sauce adheres to all sides of the cubes. Return the pan into the smoker.
8. Once the sauce has reduced and the cubes look caramelized it is time to pull from the smoker. Put the burnt ends onto a plate and top with the remaining cup of blueberry sauce. Enjoy!
9. In a saucepan combine the blueberries and apple juice. Bring to a boil. Pour the cornstarch, sugar, and cayenne (optional) into the saucepan while stirring continuously. Let the sauce thicken and reduce heat. Add the lemon juice and stir. Set aside till it is time to use on the burnt ends.
10. Serving Suggestion: Over Homemade Waffles

Pork Belly Street Tacos

Cooking Time: 4 Hrs

Ingredients:

- Pork Belly - 2 to 3 lbs
- 1 Tbsp Salt
- 2 Tbsp Coarse Black Pepper
- 1 Tbsp Yellow Mustard
- 1/2 Cup Apple Cider Vinegar
- 1/2 Cup Water
- Tortillas, Onion, Cilantro

Directions:

1. Prep your Char-Griller offset smoker to a temp of 275 F. Unwrap the pork belly and trim any excess fat or meat that is not needed. *Tip* to achieve that true Central Texas Style flavor try to use oak chunks or splits throughout your cook.
2. Combine all dry ingredients in shaker for easy application. Rub the pork belly down with mustard or a binder of your choice. Season the pork belly liberally.
3. Put the pork belly on the smoker once it is seasoned and the smoker temperature is at 275 F.
4. At the hour mark spritz the pork belly with a mixture of apple cider vinegar and water. Continue to spritz every 45 minutes until the pork belly has reached an internal temp of 165 F.
5. Wrap the pork belly in butcher paper once it has reached an internal temp of 165 F.
6. Tip: This will help with rendering the fat and preserving the bark on the pork belly.
7. Once the pork belly has reached an internal temp of around 203 F it is time to take off the pit and let rest so the juices can redistribute. Rest for 30-45 minutes.
8. Chop up the pork belly and serve in a tortilla with cilantro and onions and enjoy!

Bacon Wrapped Pork Tenderloin Stuffed With Jalapeño Cream Cheese

Cooking Time: 3 Hrs

Ingredients:

- 2 Pork Tenderloin
- 5 Jalapeno Peppers (Seeded and Minced)
- 8 Oz Softened Cream Cheese
- 1 Cup Shredded Cheddar Cheese
- 1 Tbsp Salt
- 1 Tbsp Pepper
- 1 Tsp Garlic Powder
- 12 Bacon Slices

Directions:

1. Preheat your smoker to 275 degrees. Set up with a rack and pan to collect the bacon fat drippings and cheese that may seep out. While preheating, mix together the pepper, cream cheese and cheddar cheese in a bowl. Cut a pocket into your pork tenderloins making sure not to cut all the way through. Stuff the pork tenderloins with the mixture. Season the tenderloins with the salt, pepper and garlic. Lay your bacon out flat, slightly overlapping on a piece of cling wrap and place the tenderloin on the edge closest to you. Roll up the tenderloin in the bacon Place in smoker, pocket opening side up and smoke for 3 hrs.

Smoked Chili Hotdogs

Cooking Time: 20-30 Min

Ingredients:

- 8 hotdogs
- 8 hotdog buns
- 8 slices of cheese
- 1 cup of shredded cheese
- 1 can chili sauce
- 4 Tbsp. butter
- 1/2 Tsp. granulated garlic

Directions:

1. Place hotdog buns (whole) in a greased 9x13 pan
2. Cut hotdog sized slots with a knife
3. With finger, pack cut part of bun down
4. Melt butter and garlic
5. Baste buns with the butter and garlic mixture
6. Place a slice of cheese into each bun
7. Add some chili
8. Place the hotdog on top of the chili
9. Add more chili
10. Top with shredded cheese
11. Sprinkle with parsley flakes
12. Place on smoker at 250°F
13. Smoke for 20-30 minutes or until cheese is melted

Grilled Pork And Sweet Potato Verde Chili

Cooking Time: 3.5 Hrs

Ingredients:

- 2 Lbs Pork
- 2 Large Sweet Potatoes - Diced
- 3 Ears of Corn on the Cob
- 1 Bunch Cilantro - Stems Cut from Leaves and Set Aside
- 2 Cloves of Garlic
- 3 Tbsp Ground Cumin
- 1/2 Cup olive Oil or Avocado Oil
- 2 Cups Salsa Verde
- 6 Cups Chicken Stock
- 1 Can White Beans
- Salt and Pepper to taste
- Garnish: Cilantro, Radish, Red Onion, and/or Sour Cream

Directions:

1. Remove stems from fresh cilantro, and add to blender with garlic cloves, oil, cumin, and a pinch of s&p. Pulse until smooth and combined.
2. Preheat Char-Griller to high heat, I recommend charcoal for this recipe as it will add even more flavor.
3. In a large bowl, transfer corn, pork, and sweet potato pieces. Pour blended marinade over the ingredients and toss to combine. Once grill is heated, add all to grill, and cook until charred on each side, 6-8 mins per side. Remove and set aside.
4. Once the grilled items are cool to the touch, dice sweet potatoes and pork into similar sized pieces, and cut corn off the cob. Transfer these items to a soup pot, adding salsa verde, & chicken stock. Bring to a simmer over low.
5. Add ½ cup chopped cilantro leaves, the white beans, and S&P to taste. Simmer on low partially covered for 3 hours, until pork is fall apart tender, and chili has thickened. Serve with garnishes of choice and enjoy! Leftover Chili can stay in the fridge for up to 7 days, and frozen for 6 months.

Bone-in Pulled Ham

Cooking Time: 8 Hrs

Ingredients:

- 12-15 lb. bone-in ham
- 2-20 oz. cans of crushed pineapple
- 4 C. brown sugar
- 6 Tbsp. mustard

Directions:

1. Get smoker ready and set at 250°F.
2. Place ham in an aluminum pan or cast-iron Dutch oven
3. Divide marinade in half, and pour one half marinade over top of ham
4. Place ham in smoker and baste hourly
5. Cook for around 8 1/2 hours, until ham reaches internal temp of 160°F
6. Remove ham from smoker and cover with foil for 1-2 hours
7. Shred ham and place in slow cooker or stock pot, adding juice and drippings from pan
8. Add additional marinade and pour over top of ham, mixing well
9. Cook for 1 hour until marinade is fully incorporated into shredded ham
10. All done! Makes good sandwiches or great to eat alone!

DESSERTS

Cheesecake Stuffed Apples

Cooking Time: 60 Min

Ingredients:

- Medium Baking Apples (I used Pink Lady) - 4
- Softened Cream Cheese - 8 Ounces
- Egg - 1
- Sugar - 1/3 Cup
- Cinnamon - 1/4 Teaspoon
- Crushed Graham Crackers - 1/4 Cup
- Prepared Caramel Sauce for Garnish

Directions:

1. Light AKORN and heat to 325
2. Cut bottoms of apples just enough to make them stand up straight
3. Hollow out apples with an apple corer or melon baller. Leave a ¼ inch of flesh around sides and bottom
4. Mix cream cheese, egg, sugar, vanilla, and cinnamon together until smooth
5. Spoon cream cheese mixture into each apple, leaving 1/2 inch space at the top
6. Sprinkle tops with graham crackers
7. Place apples in a small aluminum pan and place on grill
8. Allow to bake for 50-60 minutes. Filling should look semi set and apples should be soft
9. Allow to cool at room temperature then place in refrigerator until cold
10. Before serving, drizzle with caramel sauce

Smoked White Chocolate Christmas Candy

Cooking Time: 1 Hrs

Ingredients:

- 3 Cups Cheerios
- 3 Cups Corn Chex
- 3 Cups Peanut Butter Chex
- 1 Cup Butter Snaps Pretzels
- 1.5 Cups M&Ms
- 32 oz white Chocolate Chips

Directions:

1. Smoke white chocolate chips using your Char-Griller Offset charcoal smoker.
2. Add 6 lit charcoals to the far side of firebox along with a mild smoking wood chunk. Maple wood goes well with this recipe. Feel free to leave vents fully open.
3. You will need 2 foil baking pans. Fill pan number one with a layer of ice cubes. About ¼ of the way full. Add white chocolate chips to the second pan. Place pan with white chocolate on top of the pan with the ice.
4. Place stacked pans in cooking chamber of your smoker. Keep as far away from fire box side as possible.
5. Smoke for 30-45 minutes. For a milder smoke flavor try 30 minutes. To impart a stronger smoke flavor, try 45 minutes.
6. Melt white chocolate over heat source.
7. Add white chocolate to a large saucepan or keep in foil pan.
8. Over medium heat or lit coals, melt until white chocolate is a smooth consistency able to be drizzled. Be sure to stir often and do not over melt.
9. In a large mixing bowl or 2 foil pans, combine dry ingredients (cheerios, corn chex, peanut butter chex, pretzels, and m&m's) making sure to evenly distribute the ingredients.
10. Drizzle white chocolate on the dry mixture. Stir in making sure to coat all the mixture in the white chocolate.
11. Lay out on parchment paper or leave in foil pans as a nice thin layer to dry/cool for 1 hour.
12. Break into small to medium pieces and enjoy!
13. This stores well in the fridge and the freezer!

Bourbon Glaze For Candied Bacon Scones

Cooking Time: 15 Min

Ingredients:

- Bourbon - 3 Tbsp
- Vanilla - 1 tsp
- Powdered Sugar - 2 cups
- Milk - 4 Tbsp

Directions:

1. Place all ingredients in a small pan and stir to combine. Place pan on grill and allow to heat through for 15 minutes. Stir half way through. Remove from grill and cool. Open grill vents and increase temperature to 400 to cook the scones. Make the scone dough.

Grilled S'mores 4 Ways

Servings: 4

Cooking Time: 5 Min

Ingredients:

- Graham Crackers - 4 Full Crackers
- Large Marshmallows - 4
- Milk Chocolate Bar
- Dark Chocolate Bar
- Cookie Butter
- Peanut and Caramel Candy Bar
- Chili Powder
- Peanut Butter

Directions:

1. Heat grill to 350 degrees
2. Break four graham crackers in half and lay out.
3. Top the first graham cracker with milk chocolate bar and peanut butter.
4. Top the second graham cracker with milk chocolate and cookie butter
5. Top third graham cracker with dark chocolate and a sprinkle of chili powder.
6. Top fourth graham cracker with Snickers Bar cut in half longways.
7. Top each graham cracker with a marshmallow and the other half of the graham cracker.
8. Wrap each s'mores in its own foil packet.
9. Place on warming rack of the grill for 4 to 5 minutes.
10. Enjoy.

Deep Dish Apple Pie

Cooking Time: 40 Min

Ingredients:

- 8 medium tart apples, cored, peeled and sliced (makes 10 C.)
- 2 C. and 3 Tbsp. all-purpose flour
- ½ C. shortening
- 2 large eggs
- ¼ C. cold water
- 2 Tbsp. apple cider vinegar
- 1 Tsp. lemon juice
- ¼ C. sugar
- ¼ C. brown sugar
- 1 Tsp. ground cinnamon
- ½ Tsp. ground nutmeg
- 1 Tbsp. milk
- Unsalted butter, softened

Directions:

1. Pre-heat grill to 350°. Add 2 C. flour to a large bowl and cut in shortening. Mix until crumbly.
2. In a small bowl, whisk 1 egg, water and apple cider vinegar together and gradually add to crumb mixture, tossing with a fork until dough holds together when pressed.
3. Shape into a ball and wrap in plastic. Refrigerate 30 minutes or overnight, if desired.
4. Filling: In a large bowl, toss apples with lemon juice, sugars, remaining flour, cinnamon and nutmeg until evenly coated. Arrange in a single layer on a baking sheet. 2. Place pan onto grill and bake at 350°F with lid closed for 10-15 minutes, until apples release their juices. 3. While apples are baking, turn dough out onto a floured surface and roll into 2 circles large enough to cover a buttered pie dish with an overhang of at least 1". Place 1 dough into pie dish and prick the bottom with a fork. 5. Remove apples from grill and place evenly into prepared pie dish. Place the other pie dough on top of the apples and crimp the edges. 6. In a small bowl, whisk 1 egg together with milk to make egg wash and brush over pie. Cut slits in top. 7. Bake at 350°F for 40 minutes or until crust is golden brown. Remove from grill and run a knife around the side of the pan to loosen pie.
5. Cool on a wire rack and serve with ice cream, if desired. Enjoy!

Akorn Cinnamon Streusel Coffee Cake

Cooking Time: 2 Hrs

Ingredients:

- 1 ½ cups all-purpose flour (Topping)
- 1 ¼ cups packed light-brown sugar (Topping)
- 1 ½ tsp ground cinnamon (Topping)
- 1 ½ sticks cold salted butter, cut into fifths (Topping)
- 1 ½ cups chopped toasted pecans (Topping)
- 1 tsp kosher salt (Topping)
- 1 ¼ tsp baking powder (Cake)
- ½ tsp baking soda (Cake)
- 1 stick salted butter (room temperature) (Cake)
- 2 cups all-purpose flour (Cake)
- 1 ¼ cup granulated sugar (Cake)
- ½ tsp kosher salt (Cake)
- 2 large eggs (Cake)
- 1 ½ tsp vanilla extract (Cake)
- 1 cup plain greek yogurt (Cake)
- 1 cup powdered sugar (Glaze)
- 2 tbsp milk (Cake)

Directions:

1. Oktoberfest doesn't have to be just brats and sauerkraut. Bryan Head, @thebbqhead, made a classic Cinnamon Streusel Coffee Cake recipe and used his AKORN to bake it!
2. Toast pecans. Preheat oven to 275°F. In a bowl, melt a half stick of salted butter and toss pecans in the butter. Lay out pecans evenly on a baking sheet and toast for one hour flipping every 15 minutes. Let cool. Chop coarsely and set aside. Make the streusel topping. Mix together flour, ¾ cup brown sugar, 1 tsp cinnamon, and 1 tsp of salt. Cut in butter with sturdy fork or rub in with your fingers until pea-sized clumps remain. Mix in ½ cup chopped pecans. Refrigerate until ready to use. Make the streusel center. Mix together remaining ½ cup brown sugar, ½ tsp cinnamon, and 1 cup pecans. Prepare AKORN for indirect heat at 325°F. Make your cake: Butter the pan. Use a 9-inch tube pan with a removable bottom for best results. Sift in flour, baking powder, baking soda, and ½ tsp salt into a mixing bowl. Beat butter and granulated sugar with a mixer on medium speed for 2 minutes. Beat in eggs, one at a time, then vanilla. Beat in flour mixture in 3 stages alternating with greek yogurt, beginning and ending with the flour. Continue to beat at medium speed until well combined. Add half the batter into the pan. Sprinkle on the streusel center mixture evenly. Add the rest of the batter and spread evenly using a spatula. Sprinkle on the streusel topping evenly over batter. Bake until cake shows golden brown and a toothpick inserted into the center comes out clean, about 1 hour. Transfer pan to a wire rack to cool. Remove cake from pan. Make the glaze: Mix together powdered sugar and milk until you get your desired consistency. Drizzle over cake and down the sides and middle. Slice and enjoy!

Glazed Oatmeal Raisin Cookies

Cooking Time: 15 Min

Ingredients:

- 2 C. oats
- 2 C. all-purpose flour
- 1 Tbsp. baking powder
- 2 Tsp. cinnamon
- ½ Tsp. nutmeg
- 1 Tsp. salt
- 2 sticks unsalted butter, softened
- 1 C. sugar
- ½ C. brown sugar
- 2 eggs
- ½ C. raisins
- 1 C. powdered sugar
- 1 Tbsp. vanilla extract
- 2-3 Tbsp. milk

Directions:

1. Pre-heat grill to 350°F. 2. In a medium bowl combine the oats, flour, baking powder, cinnamon, nutmeg, and salt. Mix well and set aside. 3. In a large bowl whisk the butter, sugar, and brown sugar together until sugar is dissolved. Add in the eggs one at a time, stirring well until combined. 4. Add the oat mixture to the butter mixture and stir until combined. Fold in the raisins. 5. Drop 1 Tbsp. of cookie batter onto cookie sheets, 2" apart. Bake 15 minutes or until the edges are golden brown. Remove from grill and transfer to a wire rack to cool. 6. While cookies are cooling, prepare icing by combining the powdered sugar and vanilla in a bowl. Gradually add in milk until mixture is thick but spreadable.
2. Dunk the top of each cookie into the icing and let the excess drip off. Serve warm.

Candied Bacon Scones With Bourbon Glaze

Cooking Time: 15 Min

Ingredients:

- All Purpose Flour - 3 Cups
- Salt - 3/4 tsp
- Baking Powder - 1 Tbsp
- Sugar - 1/3 cup
- Cinnamon - 1/2 tsp
- Vanilla Extract - 1.5 tsp
- Heavy Cream - 1.5 Cups
- Chopped Bacon - 1/3 cup
- Heavy Cream - 1/4 cup

Directions:

1. Look here for the Candied Bacon Recipe and here for the Bourbon Glaze Recipe.
2. Have the Candied Bacon and Bourbon Glaze Ready nearby. Whisk together flour, salt, baking powder, sugar, and cinnamon. Add 1 1/2 c. cream, vanilla, candied bacon, and stir to combine. Divide dough in half. Flour a cutting board and pat each half into a 6" circle. Brush each circle of dough with the remaining cream. Place dough on parchment paper and cut into 6 triangles. Pull each wedge apart slightly and place in the freezer for 10 minutes. Transfer scones on the parchment paper to the grill grates. Bake for 15 minutes or until golden brown. Remove from grill and allow to cool. Using a 1/4 measuring cup, pour glaze over each scone and top with remaining chopped bacon.

Salted Caramel Chocolate Tart

Cooking Time: 20 Min

Ingredients:

- 1- 8 oz Bag of Sea Salt Kettle Potato Chips, Crushed (Crust)
- 1/4 Cup Flour (Crust)
- 5 Tbsp Unsalted Butter, Melted (Crust)
- 1 Cup Sugar (Caramel)
- 1/2 Cup Heavy Cream (Caramel)
- 6 Tbsp Unsalted Butter (Caramel)
- 1 tsp Sea Salt (Caramel)
- 10 Oz Semisweet Chocolate Chips (Chocolate Layer)
- 1/4 Cup Heavy Cream (Chocolate Layer)
- 1/4 Cup Sugar (Chocolate Layer)
- 2 tsp Vanilla Extract (Chocolate Layer)
- 2 Large Eggs (Chocolate Layer)

Directions:

1. Light grill for indirect heat and heat to 350.
2. In a large bowl, combine crushed chips, melted butter, and flour. Mix until combined.
3. Press into tart pan and place on grill. Bake for 15 minutes.
4. Remove from grill and allow to cool.
5. In a sauce pan over medium heat, add sugar and allow to melt completely, stirring frequently.
6. Add cream and butter, stir until combined.
7. Add sea salt and allow to boil for 5 minutes.
8. Remove from heat and allow to cool for 15 minutes.
9. Pour caramel onto crust.
10. In a saucepan over medium heat, add cream and allow to heat up.
11. Add chocolate chips and sugar, stir until melted and smooth.
12. Add eggs one at a time stirring until combined.
13. Add vanilla and stir.
14. Pour chocolate until crust.
15. Place tart on grill and allow to bake for 20 minutes.
16. Remove from grill and let cool.

Skillet Brownie On The Grill

Ingredients:

- Softened Butter- 2 Tablespoons
- Heavy Whipping Cream- 1 Tablespoon
- Large Egg- 1
- Erythritol Blend (or Sweeter of Your Choice)- 3 Tablespoons
- Cocoa Powder- 2.5 Tablespoons
- Almond Flour- 2.5 Tablespoons
- Pinch of Sea Salt

Directions:

1. Preheat the grill to 350°.
2. Mix together all of the ingredients until smooth and spread the batter in a greased mini cast iron skillet.
3. Place the skillet directly on the preheated grill grate, close the grill, and bake for 6 to 8 minutes—or just until set. Do not over bake in the grill, as the hot skillet will continue to bake the brownie as it sits.
4. Top with sugar free vanilla ice cream, sugar free chocolate syrup, and a sliced strawberry. Serve warm.
5. This serves one to two, but can be doubled or tripled for more servings. Bake each batch in its own mini skillet.

Guinness Cupcakes With Whiskey Salted Caramel Buttercream

Cooking Time: 25 Min

Ingredients:

- 1 Devils food Cake Mix
- 1 3.9 Oz Instant Chocolate Pudding
- 1 Cup Sour Cream
- 1/2 Cup Guinness
- 1/2 Cup of Oil
- 4 Eggs
- 3/4 Cup Mini Chocolate Chips
- 1 Cup of Light Brown Sugar
- 1/4 Cup of Butter
- 1/4 Cup of Milk
- 1/4 Cup of Whiskey
- 1/4 Tbsp Sea Salt
- 4 Sticks of Unsalted Butter
- 6 Cup of Powdered Sugar
- 1/4 Cup of Salted Caramel

Directions:

1. Heat Akorn to 325 for indirect heat and add liners to a cupcake pan Add cake mix, pudding, sour cream, oil, Guinness, eggs, and ½ c. of the chocolate chips in a large bowl and mix together until combined Divide batter evenly into 24 cupcakes Bake for 20 minutes or until middle of the cake springs back when gently pushed down or until a toothpick inserted into the center comes out clean While cupcakes are cooling, add brown sugar, 1/4 c. butter, milk, and sea salt to a medium sauce pan On medium heat, melt caramel mixture stirring frequently until mixture starts to simmer Allow to simmer without stirring for 5-7 minutes until thickened. Remove from heat and allow to cool To make the frosting, add butter to mixer and beat until smooth and creamy. Slowly add the powdered sugar and beat until light and fluffy. Add caramel to frosting and beat until combined Top cooled cupcakes with a spoonful of buttercream and spread across the cupcake I like to add a drizzle of the leftover caramel on top of the frosted cupcakes with a little sprinkle of the leftover chocolate chips
2. If caramel starts to thicken too much to drizzle, you can microwave it for 10 seconds

Grilled Pumpkin Pie With Smoked Gingersnap Crust

Cooking Time: 45 To 60 Min

Ingredients:

- 15 Gingersnaps
- 5 Whole Graham Crackers, Broken Apart
- 2 Tbsp Light Brown Sugar
- 4 Tbsp Unsalted Butter, Melted
- 1 - 15 oz Can Pumpkin Puree
- 1 - 14 oz Can of Sweetened Condensed Milk
- 1 Tsp Cinnamon
- 1/2 tsp Ground Ginger
- 1/2 tsp Nutmeg
- 1/2 tsp Ground Cloves
- 2 Eggs, Lightly Beaten

Directions:

1. Add charcoal and a handful of mesquite wood chips to AKORN. Add the Smokin' Stone and preheat to 350 degrees F.
2. Place metal tin of gingersnaps and graham crackers on the grill.
3. Allow the cookies to smoke for 15 minutes.
4. Combine gingersnaps, brown sugar and butter into a food processor and process to moist crumbs.
5. Spoon crumbs into a greased pie pan and press into pan to form crust.
6. Return pie pan to grill and cook for 10 minutes.
7. Remove and allow to cool for 10 minutes.
8. While crust is cooling, whisk together pumpkin, sweetened condensed milk, eggs, and spices until combined.
9. Pour mixture into crust.
10. If desired, place foil around edges of crust to protect it from burning.
11. Return pie to grill and cook for an hour or until a toothpick inserted in the center comes out clean.
12. Cool and serve with whipped cream.

Spooky Brain Cinnamon Buns

Cooking Time: 30 Min

Ingredients:

- One Can Cinnamon Rolls
- Strawberry Jam
- Cinnamon Roll Frosting

Directions:

1. Layer the dough in a pan up against each other in and shaped it to look like a brain.
2. Heat oven or grill to 350°
3. Bake the cinnamon rolls for 30 minutes
4. While the cinnamon buns are baking, add the strawberry fruit spread to the icing and mixed it.
5. Then add the icing on to the cinnamon buns when they are done baking.

Strawberry And Rhubarb Crumble Pie

Cooking Time: 35-40 Min

Ingredients:

- 1¼ C. and ¾ C. all-purpose flour, plus 2 Tbsp. for filling
- 1 C. unsalted butter, diced and divided
- 1 C. sugar
- ½ C. light brown sugar
- 1 large egg
- 2 C. fresh rhubarb, cut into ½" dice
- 2 C. fresh strawberries, stemmed and sliced
- ¼ Tsp. orange zest, finely grated, optional
- 2 Tbsp. cold water, or more as needed
- 1 Tsp. vanilla extract
- Cold water, as needed

Directions:

1. Add 1¼ C. flour and salt to a large bowl and cut in ½ C. of butter with a pastry blender until the mixture resembles coarse crumbs. 2. Gradually add cold water to crumb mixture, until dough holds together when pressed. 3. Shape into a ball and wrap in plastic. Refrigerate 30 minutes. 4. Turn dough onto a floured surface and roll into a circle large enough to cover a buttered pie dish. Place dough into pie dish, trim the edges and prick the bottom with a fork.
2. Crumble Topping
3. In a medium bowl, combine ¾ C. flour, light brown sugar, and remaining ½ C. of butter Mix using a pastry blender or electric mixer until it resembles coarse crumbs.
4. Filling:Pre-heat grill to 400°F. In a large bowl, whisk 2 Tbsp. flour, egg, 1 C. sugar and vanilla together, until sugar is dissolved. 2. Add strawberries and rhubarb and mix until just blended. Let stand for 30 minutes at room temperature. 3. After 30 minutes, pour filling into pie crust. Sprinkle crumble topping evenly over pie and cover loosely with foil. Bake at 400°F for 35-40 minutes or until filling is bubbly and crumble topping is golden brown. Remove foil during the last 10 minutes.
5. Cool on wire rack before slicing and serving.

Plum Galette

Cooking Time: 45-50 Min

Ingredients:

- 1½ C. and 3 Tbsp. all-purpose flour
- 1 ½ sticks unsalted butter, cut into ½" pieces
- ¼ Tsp. salt
- 1/3 C. ice water
- ¼ C. plus 1/3 C. sugar, reserve 1 Tsp.
- 3 Tbsp. ground almonds
- 2½ lbs. large plums, halved, pitted and cut into ½" wedges
- ½ C. good-quality plum preserves, strained if chunky or seedy
- Corn meal, for dusting

Directions:

1. Put 1½ C. flour, butter and salt into a food processor and mix for 5 seconds. 2. Add ice water and mix for 5 seconds longer, just until the dough holds together. Small pieces of butter should still be visible. 3. Remove the dough and gather it into a ball. On a lightly floured surface, roll out the dough into a large circle, 1/8" thick. 4. Drape the dough over the rolling pin and transfer to a large baking sheet. Refrigerate the dough until firm, 10-20 minutes. 5. While dough is chilling, pre-heat grill to 400°. In a small bowl, combine ¼ C. of the sugar with the ground almonds and 3 Tbsp. flour and mix well. Spread evenly over the dough to within 2" of the edge. 6. Arrange plum wedges on top and dot with butter. Sprinkle 1/3 C. sugar over the fruit. Fold the edge of the dough up over the plums to create a 2" border.
2. Tip: If the dough feels cold and firm when folding up the edges, wait a few minutes until it softens to prevent cracking.
3. Sprinkle the border with the remaining 1 Tsp. sugar. 7. Transfer the galette to a pre-heated pizza stone dusted with corn meal to prevent sticking, and bake at 400°F for 45-50 minutes, until the fruit is very soft and the crust is golden brown. 8. Remove from the grill and evenly brush the preserves over the hot fruit.
4. Allow the galette to cool before slicing and serving. Enjoy!

Candy Jar Brownies

Cooking Time: 25 Min

Ingredients:

- 20 Tablespoons Butter (Unsalted)
- 2 Cups White Sugar
- 1 Teaspoon Vanilla
- Four Large Eggs
- 1.5 Cups Unsweetened Cocoa Powder
- 1 Cup All Purpose Flour
- 2 Tablespoons Espresso Powder
- One Tablespoon Salt
- Variety of Candy (About 3 Cups)

Directions:

1. We didn't stop there. We also decided to cook it on the Char-Griller AKORN Kamado Grill because it is so versatile. The chocolate smell plus charcoal...we were in heaven. Before you start, check out our Guide to Baking on the AKORN.
2. Preheat AKORN to 350°F.
3. Cut up a variety of candy bars. Place in individual bowls.
4. Unwrap candy pieces that have foil and add those to individual bowls.
5. In a large bowl, cream together butter and sugar with hand mixer. Mix for 3 minutes.
6. To creamed butter and sugar, add vanilla and eggs. Mix together.
7. Sift four and cocoa into the bowl with the wet ingredients.
8. Add espresso powder and salt. Mix everything together.
9. Note: This mixture will be extremely thick. This is okay. The chocolate from the candy will melt, adding extra moisture to the brownie.
10. Butter baking pan. We used a foil pan so it wouldn't get smoke stains, but any 11 by 9 pan will do.
11. Add 1/3 of the brownie mixture to the bottom of the pan. Spread evenly.
12. Add 1/3 of the candy. (We used the Lava Cake Hersey Kisses and Heath Bar Pieces).
13. Add the second third of the brownie batter. Spread as evenly as you can.
14. Add the second third of the candy. (We used Hersey Cookie Bar and Butterfinger pieces)
15. Add the final layer of brownie batter. Spread evenly.
16. Add the final pieces if candy to decorate the top. (We used Reeses Hearts and M&Ms).
17. Bake on the AKORN for 20 to 25 minutes. Use a toothpick to test if it is done.
18. Cool, cut into pieces and enjoy!
19. Note: Use both the vents to adjust the temperature on the AKRON. More closed vents will help it cool down, open vents will help it heat up. Airflow is key.

OTHER FAVORITE RECIPES

Hassleback Potatoes

Cooking Time: 25 Min

Ingredients:

- 6 Russet Potatoes
- 1 Pack of Cheddar Cheese Slices
- 1 Pack of Pepper Jack Slices
- Chipotle Powder
- Oregano
- Salt and Pepper to Taste
- Cooked Bacon (Diced)
- Chives (Sliced)
- Sour Cream

Directions:

1. Set up the Flavor Pro for indirect cooking. Ignite burners and turn to medium high. Cut thin slices in the width of the potatoes, but be careful to not slice all the way through. Wrap the potatoes in foil and place on the side of the grill away from the burners. Allow to cook until tender. About 45 minutes to an hour. Remove potatoes from grill and unwrap. Place alternating slices of cheddar and pepperjack in the potato. Season potatoes with chipotle powder, salt, pepper, and oregano. Place potatoes back on the grill unwrapped for 10 to 12 minutes or until cheese is melted. Garnish with bacon, chives, sour cream and serve.

Flat Iron Sundried Tomato Omelet

Cooking Time: 10 To 15 Min

Ingredients:

- 2 to 3 Eggs
- 2 Tbsp Milk
- 1 Tbsp Sundried Tomatos
- 1 to 2 Slices Diced Ham
- 1/8 Cup Mozzarella Cheese, Shredded
- Fresh Basil, Chopped
- Salt and Pepper to Taste

Directions:

1. Whisk together eggs, milk, and salt and pepper
2. Preheat griddle to medium high and add desired oil
3. Pour egg mixture on griddle using the spatulas to make sure it doesn't spread too much.
4. Allow to cook for 2 to 3 minutes and add in tomatoes, cheese, ham and basil to one side of the omelet and use the spatula to fold over the other side to make the omelet.
5. Turn down the burner to medium low and allow to cook until cheese is melted, flipping once.

Smoked Bone-in Pork Shoulder Steak

Cooking Time: 2 Hrs

Ingredients:

- Bone-in Pork Shoulder Steaks (1 1/2 to 2 in. thick) - 2
- Char-Griller Rib Rub- To Your Tasting
- Cranberry Juice - 1/2 Cup
- BBQ Sauce - 1/2 Bottle
- Apple Wood/Charcoal

Directions:

1. Season both sides of the pork steaks liberally with Char-Griller Rib Rub. Set aside and to allow the steaks to marinate. Begin prepping the fire to 275 F. *Tip* Put a water pan inside your smoker to allow for extra moisture.
2. Once the smoker has reached 275 F put the pork steaks onto the grill and let the smoker do the work.
3. Around the 45-minute mark pull the steaks and wrap individually with foil and add ¼ of the cranberry juice to each foil packet. Put back on the smoker at 275 F.
4. Once the steaks reach around 198 F take them out of the foil packet and sauce with your favorite BBQ sauce. Put back in smoker for another 10 minutes to let the sauce settle.
5. Pull the steaks from the grill and let rest for 10 minutes. Serve and enjoy!

Ken's Famous Baked Beans

Cooking Time: 2 Hrs

Ingredients:

- ½ lb. bacon
- 1 large sweet onion, chopped
- 1 lb. cans of baked beans
- 1 Tbsp. minced garlic, or to taste
- ½ Tbsp. smoked paprika
- 1 C. brown sugar
- 3 Tbsp. Worcestershire sauce
- 2 Tbsp. prepared mustard

Directions:

1. Drain liquid from baked beans and pour into a large cast iron skillet.
2. Fry bacon in batches, if needed, in a pan to desired crispness according to package directions, drain grease (reserving 2 Tbsp.) and crumble when cool. Set aside in a medium bowl. Do not wipe pan.
3. Sauté onion and garlic in the same pan with reserved bacon grease until tender, about 5-7 minutes.
4. Add crumbled bacon and stir in minced garlic, brown sugar, Worcestershire sauce and mustard.
5. Transfer all ingredients to cast iron skillet with beans and mix well.
6. Place on the grill at 325°F and smoke uncovered for 2 hours.

Smoked Rib Chili

Cooking Time: 7 Hrs

Ingredients:

- 2 Racks of Baby Back Ribs
- 1 Tbsp Dark Chili Powder
- 1 Tbsp of Black Pepper
- 1 Tsp of Kosher Salt
- 1/2 Tsp of Onion Powder
- 1/2 Tsp of Garlic Powder
- 1/2 Tsp of Paprika
- 1-12 oz can of Pepsi (or coke)
- 1 Large Yellow Onion (Diced)
- 1 Red Bell Pepper (Diced)
- 1 Large Jalapeno (Diced)(Optional Heat)
- 1 Tbsp of Chili Powder
- 1/2 Tbsp pf Dark Chili Powder
- 1/2 Tsp of Cayenne Pepper (Optional)
- 1/2 Tsp of Garlic Powder
- 1/2 Tsp of Kosher Salt
- 1/2 Tsp of Crushed Red Pepper flakes
- 3 15 Oz cans of Black Beans (juices drained, do not rinse)

Directions:

1. Remove the membranes from the racks of ribs and discard. Cut the 2 racks in half, making a total of 4 half racks of ribs. In a gallon freezer ziploc bag, combine all of your marinade ingredients. Put the racks of ribs in the freezer bag and seal the bag. Move the ribs around with the marinade to mix the ingredients all together and cover all surfaces of your ribs. Put the bag in the fridge and let marinade for at least 4 hours (overnight is prefered for this recipe). The next day (or after 4 hours) remove the bag and get your Char-Griller Offset smoker up to a temperature of 250 degrees F. Place the racks of ribs on the grates of the smoker and smoke with the indirect heat until you get the bark/color you desire (approx 2 hours, give or take a half an hour). While your ribs are cooking, put together your pot. Start with a cast iron skillet (or a medium/large sauce pan) and spray with your cooking oil. Add the 2 pads of butter and start to melt. To that, add your diced Onion, Bell Pepper and Jalapeno. Cook the veggies until fragrant and the onion becomes translucent (Season with salt and black pepper to taste). Remove from heat and put into a bowl, set aside. Next, in a large stock pot, add all of your powdered ingredients, sauteed veggies, black beans, tomato paste, crushed tomatoes, diced tomatoes with green chiles, and the guiness beer. Stir to combine and place the pot in the smoker with the ribs. After you get your ribs to the color/bark that you want, wrap your ribs in aluminum foil tightly and place back on the smoker. This is when you will cook for tenderness. Bring the smoker temps up to around 275-280 degrees F and cook until ribs are probe/fork tender (approx 2-3 more hours). Pro Tip: You can test doneness with the ribs by pulling on one of the bones. If it starts to slide out of the meat easily, they are done. Once the ribs are

probe/fork tender, remove from smoker and allow to rest for approximately 30 mins to 1 hour. Remove the bones (they should pull right out) and shred/cut/dice the rib meat and add to your pot. Stir everything together to combine. You're DONE!! :) Nothing left to do but garnish with some sour cream, finely diced green onions and some shredded cheese!! Enjoy!!

Fried Chicken On The Grill

Cooking Time: 20 Min

Ingredients:

- 4 Boneless Skinless Chicken Breasts
- 4 Tbsp Sucklebusters Clucker Dust
- 1/2 Cup Pork Panko

Directions:

1. Preheat grill to 325F. Cut chicken breast in half, place in bowl, add seasoning and mix well. Add pork panko and mix well. Place on grill over direct heat, flipping occasionally until chicken probes at least 165F internal. (I tend to take my chicken to 175F) Remove from grill, serve and enjoy!

Gravity 980 Quick N' Fast Grilled Vegetables

Cooking Time: 5 Min

Ingredients:

- 1 Large Zucchini (Sliced)
- 1 Large Summer Squash (Sliced)
- 1 Red Bed Pepper (Sliced)
- 3 Large Portobello Mushrooms (Sliced)
- 1 Red Onion (Sliced)
- Kosher Salt
- Black Pepper
- 1 Tbsp of Garlic Powder
- 1 Tsp of Paprika
- 1 Tbsp of Italian Seasoning (or your choice of herbs)
- 1/2 Cup of Extra Virgin Olive Oil

Directions:

1. Remove the fire shutter from the Gravity 980. Load the hopper and set the temperature to 400°F. In a large bowl, combine all veggies with olive oil and seasonings. Place a grill wok on the grates and close the grill, allowing it to preheat for 2-3 minutes before adding vegetable mixture. Using a silicone spatula, open the grill and stir vegetables around in the wok, repeating the process until vegetables reach desired doneness. Serve hot or warm. Enjoy!

Grilled Adobo Wings

Ingredients:

- 3-4 Lbs of Chicken Wings
- 5 Dried Chipotle Chilis
- 10 Dried Ancho Chilis
- 8 Garlic Cloves
- 1 tsp Salt
- 1/4 Cup White Vinegar
- 1/4 Cup of the Chili Soaking Liquid
- 1/2 tsp Cumin
- 1 tsp Black Pepper
- 1 tsp Oregano

Directions:

1. Destem and deseed the chiles, and place in a bowl with very hot tap water and allow to soak for 20 minutes.
2. Add the chiles and the remaining ingredients into a blender and blend until smooth. Add a splash of the water if too thick or lumpy. Marinade wings for 2 hours, up to overnight.
3. Grill over medium high heat on an oiled grill until done, about 20 minutes flipping every 5 minutes.

Brazilian Smoked N' Seared Picanha

Ingredients:

- Picanha (3-4 Pounds)
- 1 Whole Pineapple (Cut Into Squares Only Half Is Needed.)
- Brazilian Salt To Taste For The Picanha
- Habanero Sea Salt To Taste For The Pineapples
- Trompo King Meat Stacker Or Skewers
- Fogo Eucalyptus Lump Charcoal
- Char-Griller Grills Ceramic Akorn
- Char-Griller Grills Smokin' & Pizza Stones
- Char-Griller Grill Gloves

Directions:

1. Prepping Directions
2. Cut Pineapples into small squares. Only ½ of the pineapple will be needed. Rinse the Picanha using cold water and pat dry with a paper towel. Remove any loose fat from the top and bottom of the meat but don't remove off to much fat. The fat on Picanha tastes great and provides tremendous flavor to the meat during the cooking process. Slice the Picanha into two inch thick strips. Use Slice the meat diagonally going with grain. When the meat is sliced when it's done is when you slice against the grain. Apply even layer to taste of Brazilian Salt to all sides of the Picanha. Season all sides of the pineapples squares with Habanero Sea Salt to taste Using a Trompo King or Skewers, stack the Picanha curving the meat into a C shaped form and also stack the pineapples.
3. Smoking/Searing Directions
4. Ignite lump charcoal and preheat grill to 300°. Add the Char-Griller Grills Smokin' Stone & Pizza Stone for the smoking portion of the cook. Add the Trompo King or Skewers with the Picanha to the grill/smoker. Smoke the Picanha until internal temperature 125° is met, takes about 40 minutes. Remove the Trompo King or Skewers with the Picanha from the grill/smoker and set aside. Remove the Char-Griller Grills Smokin' Stone & Pizza Stone using a Char-Griller Grills Grill Glove and place under the grill/smoker. Time to sear the Picanha to internal temperature: 135° Add a bit more lump charcoal to the grill/smoker, insert the grill grates, open up the top and bottom vents to allow the grill/smoker to get hot: 420° and over. Place the Picanha onto to the grill/smoker grates for two minutes each side or until internal temperature 135° is reached. Remove the Picanha from the grill/smoker, add additional Brazilian salt to taste. Allow the meat to rest for 10-25 minutes before slicing. Slice the Picanha against the grain and enjoy

Smoked And Stuffed Meatballs

Cooking Time: 80 Min

Ingredients:

- 1.5 Lbs Ground Beef
- 1/4 Cup Pork Panko (Ground Pork Rinds)
- 1 Tbsp Favorite BBQ Spice Rub
- 1/2 Tbsp Dried Thyme
- 1/2 White Onion (Finely Diced)
- 3 Cloves Garlic (Finely Minced)
- 2 Tbsp Worcestershire Sauce
- 1 Large Egg
- 1 Tbsp Parmesan Cheese (Shredded)
- 4 Mozzarella Cheese Sticks, Cut Roughly 1/2 Square Pieces
- 1 Cup Sugar Free Barbecue Sauce

Directions:

1. While preheating, mix together the Panko, spice rub, thyme, onion, garlic, Worcestershire, egg and Parmesan cheese in a large bowl Add in the ground beef and mix until incorporated.
2. Place a ball of the ground beef mixture in the palm of your hand, flatten, and place a piece of the cheese in the center. Fold up the sides of the meat mixture to completely cover the cheese and roll into a ball.
3. Place in a large cast iron skillet. Repeat until finished. Smoke at 225 for 45-50 min until they reach a temp of 155. Remove skillet and cover the meatballs in the BBQ sauce. Put back in your smoker and continue to cook for 15-20 mins or until an internal temperature of 165 degrees.
4. Serve immediately.

www.ingramcontent.com/pod-product-compliance
Ingram Content Group UK Ltd.
Pitfield, Milton Keynes, MK11 3LW, UK
UKHW051132260726
13967UKWH00010B/3010

9 781803 202679